Super High Resolution

Nathan Ellis

methuen | drama

LONDON • NEW YORK • OXFORD • NEW DELHI • SYDNEY

METHUEN DRAMA
Bloomsbury Publishing Plc
50 Bedford Square, London, WC1B 3DP, UK
1385 Broadway, New York, NY 10018, USA
29 Earlsfort Terrace, Dublin 2, Ireland

BLOOMSBURY, METHUEN DRAMA and the Methuen
Drama logo are trademarks of Bloomsbury Publishing Plc

First published in Great Britain 2022

Cover photography by Helen Murray

A catalogue record for this book is available from the British Library.

A catalog record for this book is available from the Library of Congress.

ISBN: PB: 978-1-3503-7718-9
ePDF: 978-1-3503-7719-6
eBook: 978-1-3503-7720-2

Series: Modern Plays

Typeset by Mark Heslington Ltd, Scarborough, North Yorkshire

To find out more about our authors and books visit
www.bloomsbury.com and sign up for our newsletters.

Cast

Anna	Jasmlne Blackborow
Janet	Hayley Carmichael
Meredith	Catherine Cusack
Sammy	LJ Johnson
David	Lewis Shepherd
Becca	Leah Whitaker

Stage Management

Company Stage Manager	Aislinn Jackson
Deputy Stage Manager	Lara Mattison
Assistant Stage Manager	Josh York

Creative Team

Writer	Nathan Ellis
Director	Blanche McIntyre
Designer	Andrew Edwards
Lighting Designer	Prema Mehta
Sound Designer	Gregory Clarke
Associate Producer	Eve Allin
Intimacy Co-ordinator	Ingrid Mackinnon
Casting Director	Nadine Rennie CDG
Costume Supervisor	Male Arcucci
Production Manager	Seb Cannings
Assistant Production Manager	Natalya Scase
PR	Nancy Poole
Marketing	Sophie Coke-Steel
Lighting Programmer	Ben Cowens
Production Electrician	Laura Curd

Jasmine Blackborow – ANNA

Theatre includes: *The Breach* (Hampstead Theatre); *Othello*, *Much Ado About Nothing* (Pop-Up Globe); *After October* (Finborough Theatre); *Grey Man* (Theatre503); *Now This is Not the End* (Arcola); *Hood* (Theatre Royal Nottingham/New Perspectives); *Dracula* (New Vic).

Television includes: *Marie Antionette*, *Shadow and Bone*.

Film includes: *School's Out Forever*, *Art of Love*, *Aamir*, *The Protector*, *Daemon Mind*.

Hayley Carmichael – JANET

Previously for Soho Theatre: *First Love is the Revolution*.

Other theatre includes: *Home* (Chichester); *Why*, *The Prisoner*, *Fragments By Beckett* (Les Bouffes des Nord); *Under Glass* (The Clod Ensemble); *Beyond Caring* (Yard Theatre); *Here Be Lions* (The Print Room); *Hamlet* (Young Vic); *Bliss* (Royal Court).

Television includes: *Landscapers*, *Les Misérables*, *Witness for the Prosecution*, *Call the Midwife*, *Chewing Gum*, *Our Zoo*, *Garrow's Law*, *Viva Blackpool*.

Film includes: *Undergods*, *Casanova*, *The Tale of Tales*, *Paddington*.

Catherine Cusack – MEREDITH

Theatre includes: *Spring Awakening* (Almeida); *The Tempest* (Storyhouse, Chester); *The Shadow Factory* (Nuffield, Southampton); *Out of This World* (Mark Murphy's VTOL); *Dancing at Lughnasa*, *How Many Miles to Babylon?*, *The Crucible* (Lyric, Belfast); *The Seagull* (Headlong tour); *All That Fall* (Jermyn Street Theatre and 59E59 New York); *Bingo* (Chichester/Young Vic); *The Two Character Play* (Jermyn Street/Provincetown, USA); *The Early Bird*, *The Gigli Concert* (Finborough); *Judith: A Parting from the Body*, *Fragile*, *Factory Girls* (Arcola); *Uncle Vanya* (Wilton's); *Mary Stuart* (National Theatre of Scotland); *The Venetian Twins* (Watermill); *Bronte*, *The Mill on the Floss* (Shared Experience); *Blood Red Saffron Yellow* (Drum, Plymouth);

Our Lady of Sligo (NT/Out of Joint); *Mrs Warren's Profession* (Lyric Hammersmith); *Phaedra's Love* (Gate).

Television includes: *Endeavour, Hollyoaks, The Last Days of Anne Boleyn, Doctors, Jonathan Creek, Ballykissangel, The Bill, Cadfael, Coronation Street, Doctor Who.*

Film includes: *Finding Neverland, Conspiracy of Silence, Boxed, The Lonely Passion of Judith Hearne.*

LJ Johnson – SAMMY

Theatre includes: *He Said She Said* (Synergy Theatre Company); *Leather Boys* workshop (Turbine Theatre).

Television includes: *Midsomer Murders, Doctors.*

Film includes: *Que Sera, BLINKERS.*

Theatre whilst at drama school included: *Sonny, Pravda, A Streetcar Named Desire, The Radicalisation of Bradley Manning.*

Lewis Shepherd – DAVID

Lewis recently graduated from Rose Bruford College. He was a Spotlight Prize Nominee for 2022 and is the founder of arts collective INCEPT COLLECTIVE. *Super High Resolution* is Lewis's debut.

Leah Whitaker – BECCA

Theatre includes: *Love All* and *For Services Rendered* (Jermyn Street Theatre); *Alligators* (Hampstead); *An Audience with Jimmy Savile* (Park Theatre); *Love's Labours Lost* (RSC/West End); *The Christmas Truce* (RSC); *Taming of the Shrew* (Globe Theatre/tour); *Forever House* (Drum, Plymouth); *Charley's Aunt* (Menier Chocolate Factory); *Don Juan Back from the War* (Finborough); *Earthquakes in London* (Headlong); *The Heretic* (Royal Court); *Counted* (national tour); *Pride and Prejudice*

(Theatre Royal Bath/tour); *Found in the Ground* (Wresting School); *Harvest* (Oxford Playhouse/tour).

Television includes: *Whitechapel*, *Eggbox*, *Father Brown*, *Casualty*, *Holby City*, *EastEnders*, *Midsomer Murders*.

CREATIVES

WRITER
Nathan Ellis

Nathan was a member of the Royal Court Invitation Writers' Supergroup 2018–19. He is a current member of the BBC Drama Room 2021–22. His play *work.txt* received five stars in the Guardian and was Offie-Nominated in 2022. His play *No One Is Coming to Save You* ('a blazing debut' The Stage) toured the UK in 2018. He is represented by Giles Smart at United Agents and is based between London and Berlin.

DIRECTOR
Blanche McIntyre

Theatre includes: *All's Well That Ends Well*, *Titus Andronicus*, *The Two Noble Kinsmen* (RSC); *The House of Shades*, *Hymn*, *The Writer* (Almeida); *Botticelli in the Fire* (Hampstead Theatre); *Tartuffe* (National Theatre); *The Norman Conquests* (Chichester Festival Theatre); *Noises Off* (Nottingham Playhouse); *Welcome Home, Captain Fox!* (Donmar Warehouse); *The Oresteia* (HOME, Manchester); *Measure for Measure*, *Bartholomew Fair*, *The Winter's Tale*, *As You Like It*, *The Comedy of Errors* (Shakespeare's Globe); *Arcadia* (English Touring Theatre); *Women in Power*, *Tonight at 8:30*, *The Nutcracker* (Nuffield Southampton Theatres); *Ciphers* (Out of Joint/ Bush Theatre/ Exeter Northcott); *The Birthday Party* (Royal Exchange Theatre); *The Seagull* (Headlong/ Nuffield Southampton Theatres/ Derby Theatre); *Accolade*, *Foxfinder* (Finborough Theatre); *When Did You Last See My Mother?* (Trafalgar Studios).

Opera includes: *Tosca* and *The Marriage of Figaro* (both ETO).

SET AND COSTUME DESIGNER
Andrew D. Edwards

Forthcoming credits include: world premiere of *Romeo Und Julia* (Director & Creative Director – Berlin 2023); *Fack Ju Göthe* (Set Design, Berlin), *Natasha, Pierre and the Great Comet of 1812* (Set Design, Landestheatre Linz, Austria).

Theatre credits include: *Anastasia* (Director & Designer – Landestheatre Linz, Austria); *The Barber of Seville* (Sante Fe Opera); Ku'damm 56 (World Premiere, Berlin); *A Midsummer Night's Dream*, *The Tempest*, *As You Like It* (Shakespeare Globe on Tour); *La Puce À L'oreille* (Comédie-Française, Paris); *Fack Ju Göhte* (Werk 7, Munich, Stage Entertainment); *Madame Favart* (Opera Comique, Paris); *The Barber of Seville* (Grange Festival); *Così Fan Tutte* (Central City Opera); *La Bohéme*

(Opera Holland Park); *Tartuffe* (Theatre Royal Haymarket); *Après La Pluie* (Théâtre du Vieux-Colombier, Paris); *The House Of Bernarda Alba* (Comédie-Française, Paris); *Dry Powder, Labyrinth, Donny's Brain* (Hampstead Theatre); Shakespeare's Globe on Tour: 2019 (Globe on Tour); *Twelfth Night, The Taming of the Shrew, The Merchant of Venice* (Globe on Tour); *Romeo and Juliet* (Shakespeare's Globe/international tour); *As You Like It, Much Ado About Nothing* (Shakespeare's Globe); *Plaques and Tangles, Who Cares* (Royal Court); *Miss Julie, Black Comedy* (Chichester Minerva Theatre); *Blue Remembered Hills, Playhouse Creatures, Fred's Diner* (Chichester Festival Theatre & Theatre on the Fly); *Impossible* (West End/international tour); *The Life and Times of Fanny Hill* (Bristol Old Vic); *Les Parents Terribles* (Donmar Season at Trafalgar Studios); *Backbeat* (West End, Toronto & Los Angeles); *Jesus Christ Superstar* (Madrid & European tour).

LIGHTING DESIGNER
Prema Mehta

Prema is Founder of Stage Sight (www.stagesight.org). She is a Trustee of the Unicorn Theatre and an Artistic Associate at the Young Vic.

Theatre credits include: *Cruise, Mad House, The Comeback, A Day in the Death of Joe Egg* (West End); *Last Days* (Royal Opera House); *The Winter's Tale* (Royal Shakespeare Company); *Hymn* (Almeida Theatre); *What If If Only, A History of Water in the Middle East, Superhoe* (Royal Court); *The Dumb Waiter* (Old Vic); *Swive (Elizabeth), Bartholomew Fair, Richard II* (Shakespeare's Globe. Candle Consultant); *The Taxidermist's Daughter* (Chichester Festival Theatre); *Things of Dry Hours* (Young Vic); *Studio Créole* (Manchester International Festival); *Of Kith & Kin* (Sheffield Crucible/Bush Theatre); *Fame* (UK tour/Peacock Theatre); *East is East* (Northern Stage/Nottingham Playhouse); *Talking Heads* (Leeds Playhouse); *Chicken Soup* (Sheffield Crucible); *Holes, Hercules* (Nottingham Playhouse); *Mighty Atoms* (Hull Truck); *A Passage to India* (Royal and Derngate/UK tour); *A Christmas Carol, The Wizard of Oz* (Storyhouse); *The York Suffragettes, Murder, Margaret & Me* (York Theatre Royal); *Love Lies & Taxidermy, Growth, I Got Superpowers for My Birthday* (all Paines Plough); *The Effect* (English Theatre of Frankfurt); *The Electric Hills* (Liverpool Everyman); *The Great Extension* (Theatre Royal Stratford East); *The Canterville Ghost, Huddle* (Unicorn); *Wipers* (UK tour). Extended and Virtual Reality credits include: *Museum of Austerity* (BFI London Film Festival); *Adult Children* (Donmar Warehouse).

Dance credits include: *Bells* (Mayor of London 2012); *Spill* (Düsseldorf); *Sufi Zen* (Royal Festival Hall); *Dhamaka* (O2 Arena) and *Maaya* (Westminster Hall).

Event credits include: *A-List Party Area* (Madame Tussauds, London).

SOUND DESIGNER
Gregory Clarke

Theatre includes: *All's Well That Ends Well, The Two Noble Kinsmen, The Alchemist, All's Well That Ends Well, Coriolanus, The Merry Wives of Windsor, Tantalus, Cymbeline, A Midsummer Night's Dream* (RSC); *The House of Shades, Hymn, Albion, Against, The Merchant of Venice, Cloud Nine* (Almeida); *A Doll's House* (Lyric Hammersmith); *Rosmersholm, The Goat Or Who Is Silvia?, The Truth, Stepping Out, My Night With Reg, Goodnight Mister Tom, The Vortex, A Voyage Around My Father, And Then There Were None, Some Girls, Waiting for Godot, What the Butler Saw* (West End); *The Beacon, Shelter, Furniture, Richard III* (Druid); *Twelfth Night* (Royal Lyceum Theatre Edinburgh); *Admissions* (Trafalgar Studios); *The Secret Diary of Adrian Mole Aged 13 3/4* (Menier Chocolate Factory/West End); *Orpheus Descending* (Theatr Clwyd/ Menier Chocolate Factory); *Maria Friedman & Friends – Legacy, Brian & Roger, The Boy Friend, The Gronholm Method, Fiddler on the Roof, Spamilton, The Bridges of Madison Country, Lettice & Loveage, The Truth, Dinner With Saddam, Assassins, Two Into One, The Lyons, The Color Purple, Travels With My Aunt, Proof* (Menier Chocolate Factory); *A Steady Rain, The American Plan* (St James's); *Stepping Out, Henry IV Parts I and II, Jeffrey Bernard Is Unwell, Blithe Spirit, The Rivals, Hedda Gabler, The Winslow Boy, Balmoral, Peter Hall Company Season* (Theatre Royal Bath); *Welcome Home Captain Fox!, My Night With Reg, Versailles, The Night Alive, A Voyage Around My Father, The Philanthropist* (Donmar Warehouse); *The Color Purple* (Broadway), *The Twits, The Ritual Slaughter of Gorge Mastromas* (Royal Court); *All Of Us, Medea, The Doctor's Dilemma, Misterman, Tristan & Yseult* (National Theatre); *Clarence Darrow, A Flea In Her Ear, National Anthems, Six Degrees of Separation* (Old Vic); *Journey's End* (Duke of York's/ New York); *Equus* (Gielgud /New York); *Pinocchio, The Wizard of Oz, The Midnight Gang, The Watsons, A Christmas Carol, Mrs Pat, The Boy in the Striped Pyjamas* (Chichester Festival Theatre); *Annie Get Your Gun* (UK tour); *The Birthday Party* (Manchester Royal Exchange); *The Seagull* (Headlong); *Donkeys' Years* (Rose Theatre Kingston); *Arcadia* (English Touring Theatre); *The Seagull, Three Plays by Sean O'Casey, King of The Castle, The Irish Shakespeare Project, Brigit, Bailegangaire* (Druid Theatre); *The Night Alive, The Philanthropist, Pygmalion* (New York). For his work on *Journey's End* Gregory won a Drama Desk Award for Outstanding Sound Design. Gregory also won a Tony Award for Best Sound Design of a Play for his work on *Equus*.

COSTUME SUPERVISOR
Male Arcucci

Design credits include: *The Bit Players* (Southwark Playhouse), *Friday Night Love Poem* (Zoo Venues Edinburgh); *Point of No Return* (Actor's Centre), *La Llorona*

(Dance City Newcastle); *The Two of Us* (Theatre Deli); *Playing Latinx* (Camden's People's Theatre).

Costume supervisor and maker credits include: *Blues for an Alabama Sky* (as assistant, National Theatre); *The Cherry Orchard* (The Yard and HOME); *Chasing Hares* (Young Vic); *House of Ife* (Bush Theatre); *Lotus Beauty* (Hampstead Theatre); *Moreno* (Theatre 503); *The Phantom of the Opera* (Her Majesty's Theatre); *Raya* (Hampstead Theatre); and *Milk and Gall* (Theatre503).

CASTING DIRECTOR
Nadine Rennie CDG

Nadine was in-house Casting Director at Soho Theatre for over fifteen years; working on new plays by writers including Dennis Kelly, Bryony Lavery, Arinzé Kene, Roy Williams, Philip Ridley, Laura Wade and Vicky Jones.

Nadine also has a long-running association as Casting Director for Synergy Theatre Project and is a member of the Casting Directors Guild.

Credits include *Britannicus* (Lyric Hammersmith), *The Breach* (Hampstead); *Bacon* (Finborough); *Last King of Scotland, Here's What She Said To Me* and *Run Sister Run* (Sheffield Theatres); *Road* (Northern Stage); *The Glass Menagerie* and *Hoard* (Arcola Theatre); *Good Dog* (Tiata Fahodzi); *Little Baby Jesus* (Orange Tree Theatre); *Random* and *There Are No Beginnings* (Leeds Playhouse); *The Little Prince* (Fuel Theatre); *Price* (National Theatre of Wales) and continues to cast for Soho Theatre – most recently *The Ministry of Lesbian Affairs*.

TV work includes: *Dixi*, casting the first three series.

INTIMACY CO-ORDINATOR
Ingrid Mackinnon

Movement direction credits include: *Enough of Him* (National Theatre of Scotland); *A Dead Body In Taos* (Fuel Theatre); *The Darkest Part of the Night, Girl on an Altar* (Kiln Theatre); *Playboy of the West Indies* (Birmingham Rep); *The Meaning of Zong* (Bristol Old Vic/UK tour); *Moreno* (Theatre503); *Red Riding Hood* (Theatre Royal Stratford East); *Antigone* (Mercury Theatre); *Romeo and Juliet* (Regent's Park Open Air Theatre); *Liminal – Le Gateau Chocolat* (King's Head Theatre); *Liar Heretic Thief* (Lyric Hammersmith); *Reimagining Cacophony* (Almeida Theatre); *First Encounters: The Merchant of Venice, Kingdom Come* (RSC); *Josephine* (Theatre Royal Bath); *Typical* (Soho Theatre); *#WeAreArrested* (Arcola Theatre and RSC); *The Border* (Theatre Centre); *Fantastic Mr. Fox* (as Associate Movement Director, Nuffield

Southampton and national/international tour); *Hamlet*, *#DR@CULA!* (Royal Central School of Speech and Drama); *Bonnie & Clyde* (UWL: London College of Music).

Other credits include: intimacy support for *Antigone*, *101 Dalmatians*, *Legally Blonde*, *Carousel* (Regent's Park Open Air Theatre); intimacy director for *Girl on an Altar* (Kiln Theatre).

ASSOCIATE PRODUCER
Eve Allin

Eve is a producer for theatre and dance. She is Lead Producer at Broccoli Arts and Jaz Woodcock-Stewart's company, Antler. She was previously Programme Producer at Farnham Maltings. Recent credits include *work.txt* (Staatstheater Mainz); *Civilisation* (Jury Award at Fast Forward, European Festival for Young Stage Directors); *The Syrian Baker* (Farnham Maltings); *Head Set* (Pleasance); *Before I Was a Bear* (Soho Theatre).

COMPANY STAGE MANAGER
Aislinn Jackson

Aislinn is a stage manager based in London. Recent work includes: *Midsummer Mechanicals*, *Measure for Measure*, *The Taming of the Shrew*, *As You Like It*, *Henry V*, *Henry IV Parts 1 & 2*, *Macbeth* and *Emilia* (Shakespeare's Globe); *Marys Seacole* (Donmar); *Fairview* (Young Vic); *Pericles* (National Theatre); *Ink* (Duke of York's); *Queen Anne*, *The Libertine* (Haymarket) and *Dead Funny* (Vaudeville) for theatre, and *The Batman* and *Star Wars: The Rise of Skywalker* for film.

DEPUTY STAGE MANAGER
Lara Mattison

Recent theatre includes: *Bad Jews* (West End); *Much Ado about Nothing* (Shakespeare's Globe); *Two Billion Beats* (Orange Tree); *The Seven Pomegranate Seeds* (The Rose); *The Last Five Years* (West End/Southwark); *Macbeth* (Manchester Royal Exchange); *Remains of the Day* (tour).

ASSISTANT STAGE MANAGER
Josh York

Josh trained in Stage Management at the Royal Central School of Speech and Drama. Recent credits include: *King Lear*, *Macbeth*, *Measure for Measure* (Shakespeare's Globe).

Soho Theatre is London's most vibrant producer for new theatre, comedy and cabaret. Opened in 2000, bang in the creative heart of London, it is one of the country's busiest venues with a buzzing bar and a year-round festival programme with a queer, punk, counter-culture flavour. Work extends far beyond its home with a UK and international touring programme and connections; presenting shows and scouting talent at Edinburgh Festival Fringe plus close links with the Melbourne International Comedy Festival. Soho Theatre is the UK's leading presenter of Indian comedians from the burgeoning scene there and has partnerships and a Soho Theatre Comedy Producer based in Mumbai.

To create theatre we nurture new playwrights, we commission new work, we produce new plays and our prestigious playwriting award, the Verity Bargate Award, uncovers the best new and emerging writers in the UK and Ireland. Writers including debbie tucker green, Chris Chibnall, Theresa Ikoko and Vicky Jones had early work produced at Soho Theatre.

Developing digital output over time, the online platform Soho Theatre On Demand over lockdown hosted the phenomenally successful live recording of FLEABAG alongside comedy, theatre and cabaret specials. Soho Theatre now produces their own films and has more than 30 comedy specials, currently showing on Prime Video UK and the 'Soho Theatre Live' channel on British Airways inflight entertainment.

Soho Theatre is working towards the opening of an exciting new second venue, Soho Theatre Walthamstow, in 2023. A culmination of many years of Soho's work, in collaboration with a grassroots local campaign, to save a glorious, 1930s art deco venue with an incredible heritage reinvented as a 1,000-capacity venue for world-class comedy, panto, performance and participation – a 'local theatre with a national profile'.

Audience and Communications

Co-Audience and Communications Director
Peter Flynn

Co-Audience and Communications Director
Kelly Fogarty

Head of Ticketing and Sales
Mariko Primarolo

Communications Manager – Digital Content
Pete Simpson

Communications Manager – Marketing
Hannah Andrews

Communications Officer – Press
Augustin Wecxsteen

Communications Officer – Marketing
Imogen Trusselle

Communications Officer – Social Media
Laura-Ines Wilson

Audience Manager – Front of House
Holly Cuffley

Audience Manager – Ticketing
Jack Cook

Deputy Audience Manager
Sophy Plumb

Audience and Communications Officers
Lainey Alexander, Fuad Ahammed

Audiences Team
Mischa Alexander
Matthew Allen
Leeza Anthony
Erol Arguden
Brenton Arrendell
Auriella Campolina
Hamish Clayton
James Darby
Naomi Denny
Ellie-Rose Fowler
Rosa Handscomb
Andrew Houghton
Amy Ann Kemp
Chanelle King
Lee King-Brown
James Kitching
Theo Knight
Vinnie Monacello
Nancy Netherwood
Janisha Perera
Jesse Phillippi
Bethany Reardon
Ted Riley
Johnie Spillane
Ariella Stoian
Sami Sumaria
El Tooth
Esosa Uwaifo
Jade Warner-Clayton
Toraigh Watson
Joanne Williams
Ally Wilson
Cara Withers

Finance, Administration & Operations

Head of Admin & Ops / Deputy Executive Director
Catherine McKinney

Financial Controller
Kevin Dunn

Head of Finance
Gemma Beagley

Finance Officer
Declan Sheahan

Finance Assistant
Paige Miller

Facilities Manager
Stuart Andrews

Admin Assistant
Rebecca Dike

Technical

Head of Production
Seb Cannings

Technical & Production Manager
Rachael Finney

Technicians
Scott Bradley, Hannah Fullelove, Richard Gunston, Jonathan Sheffield

Soho Theatre Walthamstow

Project Director
Bhavita Bhatt

Project Manager
Simon Barfoot

Head of Communications – Walthamstow
Angela Dias

Artist in Residence
Alessandro Babalola

Executive & Project Assistant
Annie Jones

Soho Theatre Bar

Bar Manager
Rishay Naidoo

Deputy Bar Manager
Damian Regan

Bar Supervisors
Ingrida Butkeviciute, Caroline Regan, Sihaam Osman

Bar Staff
Davide Costa, Sannidhi Jain, Genevieve Sinha

Penelope Deans
Jeff Dormer
Peter Dudas
Edwina Ellis
Alice Evans
Stephen Ferns
Stephen Fowler
John Fry
Mathieu Gaillemin
Cyrus Gilbert-Rolfe
Cindy Glenn
Terry Good
Louise Goodman
Steven Greenwood
Paul Hardie
Anthony Hawser
Karen Howlett
John Ireland
Mick Jewell
Bethan Jones
Simon Jones
Sue Jones
Jen Kavanagh
Matt Kempen
Andreas Kubat Emily Kyne
Ian Livingston
Alejandra Lozada
Lucy MacCarthy
Julia MacMillan
Anthony Marraccino
Nicola Martin
Corrie McGuire
Kosten Metreweli
Rebecca Morgan
Nathan Mosher
Caroline Moyes
Mr and Mrs Roger
Myddelton
James Nicoll
Emma Norman
Sam Owen
Alan Pardoe

Helen Pegrum
Andrew Perkins
Keith Petts
Fran Plagge
Nick Pontt
Giovanna Ramazzina
Rachel Read
Charlotte Richardson
Annabel Ridley
Antonia Rolph
Laura Ross
Tamanna Ruparel
Sabrina Russow
Natalia Siabkin
Beth Silver
Sara Simpson
Michelle Singer
Heather Smith
Hari Sriskantha
Sarah Stanford
Tracey Tattersall
Sarah Taylor
Victoria Thomas
Neil Tymlin
Gabriel Vogt
Sam Webster
Mike Welsh
David Whitehead
Matt Whitehurst
Gareth Williams
Allan Willis
Geoff Wytcherley
Liz Young
Sherry Zhou
Ben Zola

Super High Resolution

For my sister Tamsin

Characters

Anna, *thirty-one, an A&E doctor*
Becca, *thirty-five, her sister*
David, *twenty-four, good-looking*
Sammy, *seventeen, Becca's stepdaughter*
Meredith, *fifty, consultant above Becca in the hospital*
Janet, *fifty, a patient*

NB: The play is set over many locations but **Anna** *should never leave the stage; scenes should blur into each other: the play should not rest.*

CW: Self-harm, suicide.

One

The entrance of a hospital – the smoking area. Night. **Anna,**
*wearing scrubs, has a bandage covering her swollen nose: her scrubs
are covered in blood. Maybe it's raining, it's definitely shit weather to
be standing outside covered in blood.*

David *stood looking at her. He's just approached, still a bit pissed
and swaying slightly – he's the last person she wants to see, so she's
got her eyes closed.*

Oh, and he's wearing a leprechaun costume.

David   You ok?

Anna   Yes.

David   Sorry. I just wanted to say sorry, that, for, that, him.
Sorry. Are you alright?

Anna   Sure.

David   Has it stopped bleeding?

Anna   Just about.

David   That's good. That's really good. He's gonna feel
awful about it tomorrow, he really is. He's a nice bloke really.

Anna   Yeah?

David   I think he just got a bit panicky. You're breathing
quite heavily?

Anna   I'm calming down.

David   He's not so good with needles. He'll definitely want
to apologise. But I think he just panicked.

Anna   Right.

David   And obviously he was fucked. So, so . . . That's . . .
Does it hurt?

Anna   Yep. Really does.

David   I broke my nose once, walked into a glass door.
Felt like a right idiot. Bet you see people who've done that
all the time?

Anna   Not really, no.

He lights up a cigarette.

Anna   I thought you came out here to apologise?

David   I did. I am. What are you doing stood out here?

Anna   Getting a bit of quiet.

David   Right. The noise in there, it's mad, I don't know
how you do it, I couldn't do it. I'd need a minute too. I
barely know him, you know.

Anna   Your brother-in-law?

David   Right. Sure. We're not mates, though. They made
me bring him in, the others, they told me I had to bring him,
but we're not friends. They're still there. At the pub.

Anna   Are you going back, then?

David   Nah. Don't think so. Just go home, I think. He just
got too drunk. Stupid prick. Thanks for looking after him,
though, really.

Anna   It's my job.

David   Yeah, but you were really nice to him.

Anna   I wasn't.

David   That must just be you, then, you must just be really
good at your job and not notice it when you're doing it
because you were, it was really nice to watch . . . not nice . . .
well, and then he hit you, but until then . . .

Anna   It was nice to watch me try to cannulate your
brother-in-law, *until* he punched me in the face?

David   Yeah. That.

Beat.

I'm going to send in feedback, about how nice you were.

Anna   Ok.

David   He'll really want to apologise, do you have an email or a number I could give him?

Anna   There's an email online.

David   Well, first thing tomorrow, I'll be sending feedback about Doctor . . .?

She sizes him up, really seeing him for the first time.

Anna   Harris.

David   Harris. Doctor Harris.

Anna   I'm not going to the police or anything, you don't have to worry.

David   No, I know, I just wanted to say thanks. And sorry. That too. For him. For that twat.

Anna   Right.

David   Ok.

Anna   Can I have a cigarette?

David   Of course. I didn't – I didn't think you did – you would, because.

Anna   I don't normally. Stressful day.

David   Take the packet.

Anna   That's ok.

David   Please. Please take it.

Anna   Ok.

David   You want something for the pain?

Anna   Are you offering me drugs?

David   No, I've got ibuprofen in my coat.

Anna   Oh. No, it's fine. I've got some, thanks. To be honest, I should probably have been more careful, he was very drunk your friend.

David   He's not my friend.

Anna   Yeah. When's the wedding?

David   Couple of weeks.

Anna   You looking forward to it?

David   Not really.

Anna   Your sister older or younger?

David   What?

Anna   The bride? Or your brother?

David   Oh. Right. I have an older sister, yeah.

Anna   Ok.

David   You?

Anna   What?

David   Married?

Anna   I don't want to answer that question.

David   Ok.

Anna   Does he normally drink like that?

David   Don't know. I didn't think so, I don't really know him, but maybe. You a big drinker?

Anna   I'm drunk right now.

David   Really?

Anna   No.

David   That's funny. You're funny.

Anna   No, I'm not.

David   You ever done stand-up?

Anna   I'm a doctor.

David   Lot of doctors do stand-up. Or write books.

Anna   Most of them do it after they leave medicine.

David   Right.

Anna   Yeah. They quit and then tell funny stories about how hard it was and how much better their life is now that they've quit.

David   You could quit?

Anna   That's true. Become a stand-up.

David   Yeah.

Beat.

You got to go back in now?

Anna   I've finished my shift, actually, three hours ago, so all done now. I was just having a minute.

David   That's good, you must be tired.

Anna   Yes.

David   I'm so sorry, again. If I make him send flowers here will they get to you?

Anna   No. Don't, it's fine, really. I hate flowers.

David   Long drive home?

Anna   I'm getting an Uber, I'm just waiting, they keep not accepting, my rating is terrible.

David   I'd offer to drive you.

Anna   But you're fucked too? I think I'll get the tube.

David   Don't want to get the tube, nutters on the tube.

Anna   Might get punched by a drunk leprechaun?

David   I'll pay for a cab.

Anna   It's fine.

David   Honest.

Anna   It's very nice of you to offer but I think I'll be alright. I'm only going up the road to my sister's. Thanks, though.

David   I'm really honestly really really sorry. Honest. That's all.

Anna   Thanks. Don't worry. Amazingly, I've had worse shifts.

David   Yeah?

Anna   Don't ask.

She goes to leave.

David   Look out for me, yeah, the feedback. It'll be really good.

Anna   Yeah.

David   My name's David, by the way.

Anna   Ok.

David   Thanks. Sorry.

Anna   Thanks for the cigarettes, David.

David   Email's online, yeah?

Anna   Yes.

David   Doctor Harris?

Anna   Yes. Anna Harris.

Two

Becca's *kitchen. It's really nice – management-consultant nice, white marble island nice (onstage this just means uplighting) – and she's got a bottle of something expensive already open. Later.*

Becca He just hit you?

Anna By accident.

Becca Christ, you look awful.

Anna It's fine.

Becca You look like you've got an abusive husband.

Anna Becca, you're not really supposed to –

Becca Oh, Christ. Is it painful?

Anna It's not that bad. It was just an accident, I was cannulating him and –

Becca Don't. No.

Anna It's not even bad. I was just –

Becca No. Please. Your work stories always start alright and then suddenly there's a placenta on the ceiling.

Anna Right.

Becca So you only just finished? God, it's an absolute, state, isn't it.

Anna What is?

Becca The NHS. You know I had a mole on my back, guess how many weeks it took to get an appointment at the GP?

Anna I don't know.

Becca It's fun, guess.

Anna I really don't want to.

Becca Just guess.

Anna   Two?

Becca   Six. Six weeks, isn't that amazing? Two! No, that'd be a miracle.

Anna   Right.

Becca   Turned out to be nothing, but, well . . .

Anna   Right.

Becca   I thought about sending you a picture of it, but you'd only have, you know –

Anna   What?

Becca   Been all, you know.

Anna   What? What would I have been?

Beat.

Becca   Lovely and sweet and nice. Just like always.

Anna   I just would have said what the guidelines tell me to say, which is to go to your GP.

Becca   Exactly. Lovely and sweet and nice. Just like always. You look absolutely dreadful.

Anna   Thanks.

Becca   You should quit. You should sue.

Anna   I'm not suing. I'm not quitting. Who would I sue?

Becca   Are you hungry, there's pecorino in the fridge.

Anna   God, you're a twat. I'm fine. Where's Will?

Becca   Running.

Anna   It's midnight?

Becca   I know. He's gone weird. Drink?

Anna   I can't drink, really, I'm on painkillers.

Becca   You can drink on painkillers.

Anna   Not the ones I'm on.

Becca   You *can* drink on them, though, they just say that.

Anna   *We* just say that, you mean. Not these ones.

Becca   I think you'll be alright.

Anna   I'm a doctor.

Becca   Alright, play the doctor card: no drink for you, then. Will's being insufferable, he went on a two-hour run yesterday. Two hours!

Anna   That's disgusting. That's actually disgusting.

Becca   I know. That's what I said. So, why not quit?

Anna   The marathon's on Sunday right?

Becca   Yes. You still coming?

Anna   Can't wait.

Becca   If you miss it, I'll garrotte you.

Anna   I said I can't wait.

Becca   You've been smoking.

Anna   Is Sammy in?

Becca   Sammy's with her mum for the weekend. Empty house, Will and I have been having a lot of sex.

Anna   Great. Good to know.

Becca   Sammy's thinking of becoming a doctor.

Anna   Is she?

Becca   Yes. So, I said you would talk to her about it.

Anna   Will I?

Becca   Yes. She'll talk to you and you'll be positive about it.

Anna   I'll lie then?

Becca   Yes. You'll lie to a teenager. Cheers, happy birthday.

Anna   Thanks.

Becca   Happy pre-birthday.

Anna   Thanks for having me.

Becca   Dad mentioned it again.

Anna   Did he?

Becca   Are you sure you can't come?

Anna   I'm working.

Becca   You could try, try again.

Anna   I did try, I've been put on, they can't move me, it's only my birthday.

Becca   He just wanted to see you.

Anna   I'll have another one.

Becca   Not our wedding, is it?

Anna   Much more important.

Becca   He's upset about it, he wanted to see you. He's never not seen you on your birthday.

Anna   How was his chest? Were his sats ok?

Becca   He's alright. You should come.

Anna   I'm working.

Becca   Well, we'll be driving if you change your mind and want a lift.

Anna   It's not about changing my mind, I have to go to work. Send my regards. And to Linda.

Becca   She's very nice.

Anna   Liar.

Becca   She's – no, she's awful. What will you do after your shift?

Anna   Nothing probably. Bed.

Becca   Have a bath.

Anna   What?

Becca   Baths are good if you're stressed. Have a bath.

Anna   My flat doesn't have a bath.

Becca   You could go to a hotel?

Anna   I'm a doctor not a fucking . . .

Becca   What?

Beat. She thinks.

Anna   Pop star.

They laugh.

Becca   Anyway, you could come here? Use our bath?

Anna   Aren't you afraid I'd wreck the place?

Becca   Would you?

Anna   Dunno. Maybe.

Becca   Will and I have been taking a lot of baths, for stress.

Anna   Bex, do you have to?

Becca   What? We have. The doctor suggested that stress could be bad.

Anna   Yes. Stress can be a common problem for *geriatric* pregnancies.

Becca   Why do you have to say that word? Why do you have to be so unpleasant?

Anna   It's a medical term.

Becca   'It's a medical term.' Go fuck yourself.

Anna   How are you feeling?

Becca   Fine. Good. We're ovulating.

Anna   Both of you?

Becca   We are.

Anna   Ok.

Becca   I've been eating a lot of nuts.

Anna   Is that good?

Becca   It has to be. Right? Nuts are good. We'll be alright, though?

Anna   Yeah.

Becca   You think?

Anna   Sure.

Becca   What?

Anna   Nothing. I've got my fingers crossed. Sounds like you're doing everything right. And there's always other options aren't there?

She lights up a cigarette. **Becca** *doesn't like that.*

Becca   If you want to smoke, smoke outside. Christ your nose looks terrible. Do you want some peas?

Anna   I'm not hungry.

Becca   Ha. It looks awful.

Beat.

Why don't you think about it?

Anna   What?

Becca   Quitting?

Anna   I like smoking.

Becca   I mean what you do, it makes you miserable.

Anna   No it doesn't.

Becca   It does, it takes over everything, and now you're getting punched.

Anna   What would I do?

Becca   Anything. Learn to crochet. You've got the money mum left you.

Anna   I like it. I like bits of it. It was a lot of work.

Becca   You're looking old.

Anna   Fuck off!

Becca   And fat.

Anna   Fuck OFF!

Becca   You are, it's the truth, your sister is supposed to tell you.

Anna   No, you're supposed to say that I'm beautiful and brilliant.

Becca   You are, of course you are, but I worry. If it's money, we can help? You could move in here?

Anna   Christ, no. Sorry. Thanks. I like my job, I like most of it, what else would I do? I don't want to be a management consultant or whatever. No offence.

Becca   None taken.

Anna   It's just tricky right now.

Beat.

Becca   Are you sleeping?

Anna   Yes. I am, yes.

Becca   Is that a lie?

Anna   I'd been thinking about seeing someone, speaking to someone, a professional.

Becca   I think that's a great idea.

Anna   Do you?

Becca   Yes. Really.

Anna   It was Mum who suggested it, actually. Before . . . Before.

Becca   Really?

Anna   Yes.

Becca   Well.

Anna   Mum was a worrier.

Becca   We're all worriers. It's in our DNA.

Anna   She said I was resilient, thick-skinned.

Becca   Like a lizard.

Anna   Fuck off.

Becca   I'm glad you're talking to someone. Just keep it in mind. You have lots of choices. And I'm here.

Anna   Yes. Thanks.

Becca   For all the non-placenta-based stories, I'm absolutely here.

Anna   Noted.

Becca   And when you talk to Sammy just say you love every fucking minute of it, yes?

Anna   Ok.

Three

An A&E cubicle. Sparse, blue light. Could be any time of the day but it happens to be the afternoon. **Janet** *is perched on the bed and has a tea towel covering her arm.*

Janet   I've been quite tired. I've not been sleeping, with the kids and everything. Yes, so I think I've been being more clumsy than usual, you know. I feel so stupid. My husband was out and it was dreadful, bit of a shock for him, you know, when he came in, you can imagine, blood everywhere, what an idiot.

Anna   Playing golf?

Janet   Yes, you know, he likes it. Couldn't for the life of me say why. Do you play?

Anna   No. You?

Janet   Not really.

Anna   Could you take the tea towel off so I can have a look?

Janet   I didn't even want to come, really, but, well, my daughter said I had to.

Beat.

I like the buggies.

Anna   The buggies?

Janet   The cars they drive in golf. I like all the accoutrements, really. The clothes, the being outdoors, the, ow, just not so much the –

Anna   Golf.

Janet   Yes, the golf aspect of golf is where I say sod it.

Anna   Does that hurt?

Janet   Not really.

Anna   It's deep.

Janet   Is it?

Anna   Your hand slipped?

Janet   While I was chopping, yes.

Anna   What were you chopping?

Janet   A potato. Dinner. Stupid, I know. No idea what happened really. Absolutely stupid, like I said.

Anna   It was your husband who came in with you?

Janet   Yes.

Anna   Do you want your husband here?

Janet   He'll come back, I just sent him away to get a cup of tea, lot of fuss, I said, so he's popped off and, well, till we get it sorted.

Anna   Sorted?

Janet   Yes, you know, sorted. Sorted out.

Anna   I'm going to have to ask a colleague to sew this up.

Janet   Oh dear. Will it take long? I don't want to bother anyone.

Anna   Shouldn't take too long. I'll give you something for the pain.

Janet   If you think so.

Anna   Are you in pain now?

Janet   Yes. I think I will. Might put me to sleep.

Anna   It might.

Janet   I could just lie down here, knock myself out, wouldn't mind. Wake me up when we land!

Pause.

Anna   Mrs Sampson, it's quite high up on your arm.

Janet   Is it?

Anna   It's in quite an unusual place. And deep, deeper than I would have expected.

Janet   He sharpens the knives, my husband, always brilliant at keeping them sharp. He has a little sort of stone that he sharpens them with. Supposed to be safer a sharp knife, isn't it, at least that's what he says, my husband.

Anna   I'm going to ask you quite a sensitive question, Mrs Sampson, if that's alright, and it's just me, and whatever you say, everything you tell me will be confidential, I won't need to tell anyone unless there is a risk to yourself or others. Ok? Is that alright? *A nod.* Did you hurt yourself on purpose?

Janet   No.

Anna   Are you sure?

Janet   Is that something people do?

Anna   Yes, it's very common and something I've had lots of experience dealing with, and there won't be any judgement or anything of that sort from me.

Janet   God, people must be very sad, musn't they to do that?

Anna   Yes. They often are.

Janet   I don't know what you want me to say?

Anna   It's just us and I'd just really like to understand what happened, so I can help you.

Janet   I'm very embarrassed. Such a silly accident. And the waiting, all those people waiting.

Anna   You're sure this was an accident?

Janet   Yes.

Anna   While you were cutting an onion?

Janet   Yes, stupid, I know.

Beat.

Anna   Ok.

She's been caught out.

Janet   Potato. It was a potato.

Beat. She's been caught out.

I didn't think he'd come back.

Anna   Your husband?

Janet   He came back sooner, it was a lot sooner, almost straight after. He forgot his golf tees, he has these special tees he's been trying out, they were on the side, if I'd have spotted them, then – Should I have done something different?

Anna   Different?

Janet   Straight down or something?

A long pause. **Anna** *takes this in but gives nothing away. She's assured and careful with her gestures and, after a pause, she speaks efficiently, like she's giving you the recipe for quite a serious Victoria sponge.*

Anna   So, here's what we're going to do, that will need stitching, ok, and then I'm going to need to call a colleague to come and talk to you about what you just told me.

Janet   What did I just tell you?

Anna   If you've been having suicidal thoughts, Mrs Sampson, that's something we are really here to help with, you're in exactly the right place, and someone from the mental health team will just be coming in to be sure we are in a really good position to help you.

Janet   Mental (. . .?)

Anna   Someone trained to offer you the help you need, yes.

Janet   Oh.

Beat.

Anna   Mrs Sampson?

Janet   I'm so sorry.

Anna You have nothing to apologise for.

Janet I'm wasting your time.

Anna You are absolutely not a waste of my time, Mrs Sampson. I am here to help you and find you the right support. That's my job.

Janet I have been quite tired. I've just been tired.

Anna Is there something the matter at home? With your husband?

Janet How old are you, doctor?

Anna I'm thirty-one.

Janet I'm old enough to be your mother. I mean this as gently as possible, I'm not sure you'd understand how complicated my life is.

Anna Perhaps not. But I'm really sure you're in the right place to get you some help. I'll get you something for the pain?

Janet Yes. Would you mind just not telling my husband?

Anna My colleague will be able to talk it all through with you.

Janet But you won't tell him?

Anna Not for the moment. If that's what you want.

Janet Ok.

Anna You're in really good hands. I'm –

Meredith *enters.*

Meredith Doctor Harris, could I have a quick word.

Anna Sorry, now's not great.

Meredith It'll only take a second. Please. Fairly urgent.

Anna   Mrs Sampson, I'll be two seconds, I'll be right back, and we'll have a chat before anyone else comes to speak to you. Do you want a tea or a water or anything?

Janet   No, I'm fine.

Anna *steps out of the cubicle.* **Meredith** *speaks at quite a lick – she's late leaving and if she delays any more the traffic will get ridiculous.*

Meredith   Anna, it's about tomorrow. I'm off now, so I needed to let you –

Anna   Tomorrow?

Meredith   Yes, tomorrow, we've moved you onto tomorrow at eight, couldn't be helped.

Anna   I'm off tomorrow.

Meredith   Yes, I know, bit of a mess-up, but we should never have had you off.

Anna   I can't.

Meredith   Why not?

Anna   I have . . . I can't.

Meredith   Why?

Anna   I have an appointment.

Meredith   You think you need your nose looking at? I think it's fine, isn't it?

Anna   Not my nose, sorry, could we talk about this later?

Meredith   No I have to go. Tomorrow's ok, though?

Anna   I was having a fairly important conversation.

Meredith   Ok, you get back to that. Email me?

Anna   I can't do tomorrow, though I have, actually, I can't do that.

Meredith   Oh, right.

Anna   I have a really important appointment. Why was it changed?

Meredith   We really need you on, it happens all the time, we're all having to do it.

Anna   I actually . . . I'm seeing a therapist tomorrow, so, it's my first session, so . . .

Meredith   I'm sure your therapist will be able to change it.

Anna   I'll get charged for it, under twenty-four hours. It's a lot of money.

Meredith   That's a shame. We really need everyone to help out. Backlogs, etc.

Anna   Could you find someone else?

Meredith   We won't get a locum now. You know how it is.

Anna   Yes.

Meredith   You don't need to cancel, you could ask them to change the appointment.

Anna   They'll still charge me.

Meredith   We really need to be all hands on deck, you know, it's such a difficult time. Perhaps you could ask them really nicely to move it.

Anna   Nicely?

Meredith   Yes, like the way I'm asking you now, nicely?

Anna   Right. Ok. That's fine. I'll come in tomorrow.

Meredith   Great. Very good. Oh, thanks so much, Anna, really appreciate it.

Anna   Ok.

Meredith   Life-saver. Really very much appreciated. Oh, and you got a message, a feedback thing, it's in the office.

Anna   Ok. I'll pick it up when I have time.

Meredith   Think it's nice.

Anna   I know what it will be.

Meredith   Nice to have good feedback, isn't it? Very nice, isn't it?

Anna   It's my birthday, as well, tomorrow, my birthday is tomorrow.

Meredith   Is it?

Even **Meredith** *can't avoid feeling slightly tense.*

Anna   Yes, tomorrow.

Meredith   Right. Alright.

Beat.

You need to get back don't you, won't keep you, see you tomorrow.

Anna   Ok.

She returns to the cubicle. **Janet** *has gone.*

Four

No time to reflect on that shitshow for too long, though, so . . .

Anna   Yes, ok.

Your son has.

Right.

You want.

No, that's not right.

Where did you read that?

Yes.

I'm not the nurse, no.

The internet?

No. That's not.

No. You probably don't.

No, I'm not the nurse.

Could I take a look?

Can I take a look?

Look at this, please.

I'm just going to

Run some tests

No, I'm a doctor

Yes, I'm the doctor

Are you

It got up there accidentally?

I'm not sure.

I'll check

I'll check

Dizziness

How are you

Fully qualified

Homeopathy isn't really

A ferret?

Keep you

The internet, right

I'll ask.

Dizziness?

Semen.

That looks

Yes.

Well, that's nice

That's

What time is it?

No, the vaccine doesn't

The consultant's busy.

Yes, it's totally safe

In your eye?

Unusual

I'm sorry you feel that.

Yes, a woman

Do you think?

Your husband?

Not your husband?

He hit you

You can tell me

We can talk

No rush

We're going as fast as we can

Fully qualified?

What?

Why?

How did you?

Yes, I am quite young, that's true

Yes

Yes

Yes

No

Because my personal number is private, unfortunately

Yes, a woman doctor

You're not going to

The baby is

The baby isn't

I know

I know

I know

Very impressive.

That's impressive.

Yep, definitely, absolutely, I'll call a 'man doctor', and you'll be waiting another six hours

Yes, still here

Still here, yes

Yep, me again

Fuck

Thank you

Thank you

Fuck

I'll just call

Fuck

That's nice

That's not

I just need to

Fuck

Yes, the consultant

No

Yes

Fuck

No

Fuck

Yes

Fuck

Fuck

Fuck

She reads the note. She smiles.

Fuck

She thinks. A bad idea forming? A good idea forming? An appallingly exciting idea:

Five

Back in **Becca***'s kitchen and* **Anna** *has a wine glass.* **David** *(no longer leprechaun) has just arrived.*

Anna   Hiya.

David   This is a nice house.

Anna   It's my sister's.

David   Is she here?

Anna   No.

David   Ok.

Anna   I came here to take a bath, my flat doesn't have a bath, she's away and then . . . She's away. Do you want a drink?

David   Sure.

Anna   I got your note. Today. Thank you.

David   I'm glad. I gave it to the other doctor, she was a bit, well, a bit.

Anna   Yeah, she's like that with everyone, actually. It was really nice. It really, well, it was nice. We don't really often get nice messages but. It really. Thanks.

David   I worried it was a bit weird, leaving my number.

Anna   It was a bit. I was a bit . . . But then I had a glass of wine and, and . . .

David   And it's your birthday.

Anna   Yeah, it is, so I thought I should have a . . . treat.

David   A treat?

Anna   The wine. Is this weird?

David   No.

Anna   Is this too much?

David   No. It's not. No.

Anna   Do you want to sit down?

David   How's your nose.

Anna   Fine. How's your friend?

David   He's fine, sends his apologies. Very red-faced in the morning.

Anna   Does he know you're here?

David   No. I didn't tell anyone. Is this legal?

Anna   What?

David   Me being here?

Anna   Yes. Probably unethical. If we had sex, that would be, that would definitely be un . . . ethical.

Oh God. Probably best if they both just ignore that she said that.

David   Right. Right. Well. Happy birthday.

Anna   Thanks. You're the first person who has said that, you know.

David   Really?

Anna   Yes. Wine ok?

David   Sure. Bad day?

Anna   Yes.

David   What happened?

Anna   Nothing. Cheers. What do you do?

David   I work for a bank.

Anna   Do you?

David   Yeah.

Anna   You're a banker?

David   Customer service. On the phones. 'Very sorry to hear that.' Lot of that. Pretty boring compared to what you do.

Anna   Sounds nice.

David   It's alright.

Anna   Sounds really nice.

David   People say I have a soothing voice.

Anna   You do. I feel soothed already.

David *goes to kiss her.*

Anna   How old are you?

David   What?

Anna   Just, how old are you?

David   Guess.

Anna   Oh, fuck's sake.

David   What?

Anna   I hate guessing, why does everyone love guessing so much?

David   I'm twenty-four.

Anna   Oh.

David   Is that a problem?

Anna (*suppressing her excitement*)   Not a problem. Not a problem at all.

David   So, what's your job like? When you're not dealing with drunk leprechauns?

Anna   You're not a virgin are you?

David   No.

Anna   Are you sure?

David   Yes. What does that mean?

Anna   Just checking. Twenty-four is quite young, you know?

David   I've been told I look old for my age.

Anna   You don't.

David   Oh.

Anna   Sorry. You asked me a question?

David   I don't know any doctors.

Anna   None?

David   No.

Anna   I basically *only* know doctors.

David   It's the same with people who work in customer service.

Anna   Really?

David   No.

Anna   Oh, right. Well, it's a lot like other jobs in some ways, a lot different in others.

David   That's clear.

Anna   Sorry, you know, but it's boring, it's like a job, any job.

David   It's a good job, though. I'm interested.

Anna   Sort of.

David   You must be smart?

Anna   Don't actually even know about that.

David   Pays well.

Anna   Not really.

David   Really?

Anna   We don't have to talk about it.

David   I want to.

Anna   It's boring.

David   I promise not to be bored.

Anna   You promise.

David   Scout's honour.

Anna   You could still be in the scouts.

David   You're very evasive, you know that.

Anna   Alright, well. So. Well, it's a good job. Sometimes. Later on it can pay well and it can be a bit easier timings-wise, but I'm a junior doctor, which means, well, it means I'm right at the bottom of the pile of shit, and it does pay well, relative to other jobs, but you don't really get paid overtime and basically everyone does a lot of overtime in hospitals, so you have to factor that in, and you have to do shift work, and you don't get a choice about holidays, so you have to miss a lot of stuff, and you have to pay for your own exams, which can cost like a grand each, even if you fail them, and you have to revise in your spare time and . . . I'm talking about exams. I really don't want to talk about exams.

David   You don't have to be at a desk, though.

Anna   You do sometimes.

David   And you get to help people. My job is a lot of getting shouted at.

Anna   Mine too.

David   Different, though.

Anna   I'm not ungrateful. I get that it seems . . . There's just a lot of . . . shit.

David   Work, isn't it?

Anna   Sure.

Beat.

No. It's. Different, isn't it?

David   How?

Anna   More dead kids, I imagine, at my work.

It's a bit uncomfortable.

Anna   Sorry.

David   That's –

Anna   That wasn't funny. I'm – fuck.

David   It's fine.

Anna   I'm nervous. I think. I'm nervous.

Beat.

David   I brought you something.

Thank God. He presents a tiny cake in a tiny box.

And.

Candle. He lights it. She's genuinely touched. As you would be; it's fucking adorable.

Wish.

She wishes. He kisses her.

Anna   I think you're gorgeous.

David   Thanks.

Anna   I do, I think you're fucking gorgeous and that was really fucking nice of you and you here just makes me want to do something disgusting, is that alright?

David   Yes.

Anna   We could have a bath? A fucking bath?

David   Sure.

She practically cheers and then kisses him. And then: **Sammy**, **Becca**'s *stepdaughter, enters.* **David** *and* **Anna** *separate.* **David** *sits down, like he's turned invisible.* **Sammy** *stands in the doorway, surprised, then amused.*

Anna   Oh, shit.

Sammy   Hi, Anna.

Anna   Shitting hell.

Sammy   I'm just going upstairs, is that ok?

Anna   Yes, yes. Becca, she, she said, my sister, she left me a key . . . So. I – I – I thought you were away.

Sammy   I was. I needed to get a folder, so, I popped back. Don't mind me, though, you carry on.

Anna   We weren't –

Sammy   What?

Anna   Nothing. Your mum didn't drive you?

Sammy   I walked.

Anna   Oh, good, that's, fine. (*Gesturing to* **David**.) This is . . .

She's forgotten his name.

David   David.

Anna   David, this is David, David, my friend. David.

Sammy   Alright, David?

David   Hi, I'm Anna's friend.

Sammy   Friend?

Anna   Yes.

Sammy   Ok. I'm Sammy. I live here.

David   Right.

Sammy   So, I'll be upstairs.

Anna   We'll be here, we're just about to, David was going. We're going.

Sammy   Ok, whatever.

She leaves.

Anna   Fuck.

David   Nice kid.

Anna   Fuck.

David   It's ok.

Anna   Fucking fuck.

David   It's fine. Really. It's fine.

Anna   Ok. You should go.

David   What?

Anna   We can't.

David   We could go? Together?

Anna   Right. We could go to yours?

David   Mine?

Anna   You cycled, right? You live close? Or not, or you could just go.

David   No, I want to. Could we go to yours?

Anna   I live miles away.

David   I don't mind.

Anna   Ok.

David   Sorry. My house is just quite shit.

Anna   I don't mind. That's fine. Or.

David   Sorry.

Anna   Don't worry. You should just go.

David   No. Let's go to yours. I'd like to. I'll order an Uber, what's your address?

She puts in her postcode. He kisses her and goes outside.

Anna   Fuck.

Sammy *re-emerges.*

Anna   That was . . .

Sammy   Don't worry.

Anna   Becca said I could come round to have . . . a bath.

Sammy   A bath?

Anna   Yes.

Sammy   For your birthday?

Anna   Right.

Sammy   And so you invited a friend?

Anna   David.

Sammy   Makes sense.

Beat.

Anna   You ok? School ok?

Sammy   Shall we not?

Anna   Ok.

Sammy   Have fun.

Anna   Ok. I'd be grateful if you didn't, if you didn't.

Sammy   Secret's safe with me.

Anna   Thanks.

Sammy   Happy birthday, by the way.

She leaves. **Anna** *considers collapsing but no time to wait:*

Six

Anna *and* **Becca** *are watching Will in the marathon. It's freezing and they both want to be elsewhere.* **Becca** *is holding her phone and looking at the tracking app thingy.*

Anna   Where is he?

Becca   He's this little dot on my phone, he's there.

Anna   Is that good?

Becca   No idea.

Anna   Is he good at running?

Becca   Very good, he says, I try to ignore him talking about it.

Anna   He's done a marathon before?

Becca   Loads of them but when I said I wasn't going to be here he was all sulky, so . . . It's nice he has a hobby, anyway.

Anna   Is Sammy coming?

Becca   Yes, in a bit, she's somewhere about.

Anna   Oh, right.

Becca   Thanks for keeping me company, though, good of you.

Anna   I'm on nights next week. I should be sleeping.

Becca   All these people, running? Amazing, really. Why wouldn't they do something fun, nice day like this?

Anna   How was it with Dad?

Becca   Fine, really good, he missed you. You could have picked up your phone.

Anna   I was working.

Becca   You could have called.

Anna   I texted.

Becca   Yeah, well. Linda made profiteroles. From scratch.

Anna   Cunt.

Becca   Yeah.

Beat.

Anna   So, Sammy's coming?

Becca   Yes, think so.

Anna   How's it going with you two?

Becca   Fine. What do you mean?

Anna   Just wondering. Do you get on? I don't really know her all that well. I haven't asked about it, so.

Becca   It's alright. She's remarkably normal, considering her mother. She's very clever, it's a bit annoying.

Anna   Did she go with you?

Becca   No. She had to stay home in the end, had homework apparently. Why?

Anna   No reason. But she's on her way?

Becca   She texted Will before he started, said she'd come find us.

Anna   I might go get coffee in a bit.

Becca   Alright.

Beat.

Showing off, isn't it, running?

Anna   Should we have made a sign, other people have signs?

Becca   I am not playing the dutiful wife holding a fucking sign.

Anna   It's a nice day, isn't it?

Becca   What?

Anna   What?

Becca   You seem happy?

Anna   Do I?

Becca   Yes. Therapist?

Anna   What?

Becca   How did it go?

Anna   Fine.

Becca   What did you talk about?

Anna   Stuff.

Becca   What stuff?

Anna   Work, therapy stuff.

Becca   Ok. That's good. We don't have to talk about it?

Anna   No.

Becca   But if you wanted to?

Anna   Thanks. Yeah.

Becca   Is work ok?

Anna   Yes. Basically.

Becca   Basically?

Anna   I had a suicidal patient run out on me.

Becca   God, Anna.

Anna   Yeah. She just left, we sent security after her but we couldn't find her.

Becca   So, what happened?

Anna   A fuckload of paperwork. I called round, tried to get her but she gave a false name. I gave a description to the police but, well.

Becca   So, that's it.

Anna   That's it.

Becca   God.

Anna   I know.

Becca   That's horrible.

Anna   Horrible.

Becca   You worried?

Anna   Yeah. A bit. Don't know. Lots of people try to kill themselves. I think it was just – She reminded me a bit of Mum.

Becca   That's hard. Did you talk about her in therapy?

Anna   Yes. I did.

Becca   Good. Did it help?

Anna   Yes.

Becca   We could talk about it? Or not?

Anna   It's fine. Let's have a nice day.

Becca   As long as you're talking to someone. And it's helping.

Anna   Yes.

Becca   Maybe you could give Dad a ring at some point?

Anna   Yeah, I meant to, I will. Maybe I'll go see him.

Becca   Really?

Anna   If I can. We could go together?

Becca   You're suggesting we could go see Dad together?

Anna   If I can get some time off, yes, what?

Becca   What's going on?

Anna   What?

Becca   What's happening?

Anna   What?

Becca   You seem good?

Anna   Yes.

Becca   Really good?

Anna   Yes. Why are you saying it like that?

Becca   Like what?

Anna   Like it's bad?

Becca   It's just, you're smiling?

Anna   I smile.

Becca   No you don't, you're a frowner, you frown.

Anna   I don't frown.

Becca   You've got horrible frown lines. I never see you smile.

Anna   Well, *you're* always there when I'm with you.

Becca   Nobody is this good a therapist. What happened?

Anna   What?

Becca   What?

Anna   What?

Intrigue: a penny drops.

Becca   You've been having sex.

Anna   No, I haven't.

Becca   You have, you're all pink.

Anna   No.

Becca   Yes. You've had some sex.

Anna   No I haven't.

Becca   Yes you have. You've got that smug look of a recently fucked person.

Anna   You're smug.

Becca   I am smug, very smug, Will and I have been at it all the time.

Anna   Becca.

Becca   This is good, great. This is good, you needed sex desperately.

Anna   Would you please stop it. You are being incredibly childish.

Becca   You're being childish. Lying about getting a quick fuck. Who was it? Go on. Tell me.

Anna   No.

Becca   You want to, there's nobody else you can tell.

Anna   I have friends.

Becca   No you don't. You missed all their weddings and now they hate you.

Anna   I missed *your* wedding and you won't leave me alone.

Becca   Who?

Anna   Is that him, where is he?

Becca   No. Who?

Anna (*forcefully*)   Nobody. Would you leave it. Please.

Becca   Alright. Fine. Keep your little secrets.

Beat.

I've got news too, you know.

Anna   What?

Becca   I was going to tell you some news.

Anna   What?

Becca   Nothing.

Anna *is outraged.*

Anna   Don't be a twat.

Becca   I'm not.

Anna   Tell me.

Anna   Is it Dad?

Becca   No.

Anna   Will?

Becca   No.

Anna   What is it then?

Becca*'s got her. Sherlock fucking Holmes. She stares* **Anna** *down.* **Anna** *caves:*

Anna   He was just some bloke.

Becca   I knew it. Some bloke!

Anna   I really don't want to talk about it.

Becca   When?

Anna   After work.

Becca *is loving this.*

Becca   When?

Anna   On my birthday.

Becca   Lovely birthday present to yourself!

Anna   Yeah.

Becca   And?

Anna   I don't want to talk about it.

Becca   Well, I do.

Anna   What's *your* news?

Becca   You going to see him again?

Anna   No.

Becca (*delighted*)   Slut.

Anna   It was just a sort of reckless sort of thing. Thought it would make me feel a bit better.

Becca   Did it?

Anna   Yes. No. A bit.

Becca   Why won't it happen again, then?

Anna   Would you just tell me what's going on?

Becca *looks at her, beaming.* **Anna** *gets that 'oh my God' feeling.*

Anna   Are you . . .?

Becca   Yes.

Anna   Really?

Becca   Yes. I went yesterday and, well, yes.

Anna   God.

Becca   I know.

Anna   Fuck. Congratulations.

They hug: actual, good news!

Becca   Thanks.

Anna   Really. Fuck.

Becca   I know.

Anna   You're happy?

Becca   Very. Really. Very.

Anna   How long?

Becca   About five weeks I think, I missed my period, so I did a test, so, yeah. Gah!

Anna   Early days?

Becca   Yes but still.

Anna   That's great. Who's the father?

Becca   Fuck off. Dad was really happy.

Anna   That's good.

Becca   Yes.

Anna   You told him?

Becca   Yes. Why? Of course.

Anna   Ok.

Becca   Why did you say it like that?

Anna   It's just early days, isn't it?

Becca   Yes, but I'm pregnant.

Anna   Five weeks, it's really early.

Becca   And?

Anna   Nothing. It's just a bit . . .

Becca   What?

Anna   Bit risky.

The joy has turned sour.

Becca   I didn't fucking tweet about it.

Anna   I know.

Becca   I didn't storm the stage at the O2 to tell people.

Anna   I know.

Becca   I'm just happy. I told my dad, our fucking dad that I'm fucking pregnant, that I'm going to fucking have a fucking baby.

Anna   That's great.

Becca   And you should be happy too.

Anna   I know. I am. I'm sorry. I've just seen a lot of –

Becca   A lot of what?

Anna   Nothing. Nothing.

A silence.

Becca   There's a coffee place just around the corner.

Anna   Do you want one?

Becca   No.

Beat.

You could just be happy for me.

Anna   I'm sorry. I am. I'm sorry.

Sammy *arrives.*

Sammy   Hiya.

Anna   Shit.

Becca   What?

Anna   Nothing. Hello, Sammy, good you made it.

Sammy   Were you apologising?

Anna   No. Yes.

Sammy   What for?

Anna   Nothing.

Becca   What?

Anna   Nothing.

Becca   Anna was going to get coffee.

Sammy   Ok. How's Dad doing?

Becca   He's that spot there.

Anna   Nice you're here, supporting your dad.

Becca   Where've you been?

Sammy   Revising.

Becca   On a Sunday.

Sammy   Well, I smoked up all my crack last night, so.

Becca   Ha. That's funny. That's part of that funny dynamic we have, isn't it? I was just saying to Anna how clever you are, wasn't I?

Anna   She was.

Sammy   Right.

Becca   Is that a new t-shirt?

Sammy   No.

Becca   Oh, ok. Tell you what, now Anna's here you can talk about her work?

Sammy   Alright.

Becca   I'm going to go and get a tea, actually, you two can chat. Do you want anything, Sammy?

Anna   We can come.

Becca   That's ok. You wait.

Anna   Could you get me a . . .

Becca *has already gone. A brief silence between them.*

Sammy   Had any more baths?

Anna   No. I. No.

Sammy   Did you have a nice time?

Anna   Yes. Shall we talk about something else?

Sammy   What do you want to talk about?

Anna   Literally anything else. Becca said you were thinking about medicine?

Sammy   Will you help me with my UCAS?

Anna   Yes. Maybe.

Sammy   I need to write my personal statement.

Anna   Have you made a start?

Sammy   Not really. I need to explain why I want to be a doctor.

Anna   Well, why do you think you'd want to be a doctor?

Sammy   Well, I've been told not to say I want to help people. Apparently everyone says they want to help people.

Anna   Is that the reason, though?

Sammy   Yeah, but everyone says that. What did you say?

Anna   The reason I gave, I think, was that I wanted to mix science and care, or something, which is sort of bollocks now, definitely was then. To be honest, it was basically because my mum suggested it. Rubbish reason.

Sammy   I like the idea of doing something where it's immediate. Where you can see the impact of what you're doing.

Anna   A lot of the time you might not.

Sammy   What should I say then?

Anna   Well, why do you think it looks interesting?

Sammy   I like biology.

Anna   That's a good reason.

Sammy   Is it?

Anna   A lot of it is very clinical. It's a very hard degree. Lot of exams.

Sammy   I mean, I don't like exams, so . . .

Anna   You don't have as much emailing as in some jobs.

Sammy   The opening line of my personal statement can't really be 'I don't like writing emails' . . .

Anna   No.

Sammy   Do you not like it?

Anna   What? Yes. Yes. It's a great profession.

Sammy   Are you sure?

Anna   Lots of people love medicine, love being a doctor. It's just about it being right for you.

Sammy   Do you see lots of horrible stuff?

Anna   Sometimes. Not lots. There's a real camaraderie working in the NHS.

Sammy   Do you ever get depressed?

Anna   No. Not more than other people. It's a very rewarding job.

Sammy   Lots of people say that about their jobs.

Anna   That's true.

Sammy   One of my mates works part-time as a dog-groomer. She's really into that.

Anna   Dogs are nice.

Sammy   You're suggesting I shouldn't apply for medicine and become a dog-groomer instead?

Anna   Well. Maybe. But, no, and if you tell Becca I said that, I'll deny it.

Sammy   She'll believe me.

Anna   You're right.

Sammy   I won't tell her. I didn't tell her about the other day. What does that bloke do?

Anna   He works at a bank.

Sammy   You shouldn't fuck bankers. They're all twats.

Anna   I'll bear that in mind.

Sammy   You should, you really should.

Anna   Can I be honest?

Sammy   Yes.

Anna   I want to be honest but Becca told me not to be honest but if you're not going to tell her, then I can be honest.

Sammy   Right.

Anna   Basically, I think you should think really seriously about it, because it's a really hard job and it eats into your life and the way the NHS is going it's only getting worse and unless you're really clear on what it entails, I think it's just really hard to advise someone to become a doctor right now.

Sammy   Ok.

Anna   You seem very sweet and I don't want you to lose that but you need to be aware that in order to be a doctor you have to, you have to push those feelings, those feelings aside, and it will: you have to, as part of the job, become numb. Which in some ways is fine, but in others is . . . not. So fine, I mean.

Sammy   Right.

Anna   But also, Sammy, honestly, if you think it's the thing you absolutely need to do, and I know this is hard to know at sixteen –

Sammy   Seventeen . . .

Anna   But if you think you *need* to do it, then I think you'd probably make a really great doctor, maybe.

Sammy   You should quit.

Anna   What?

Sammy   You quite obviously literally hate your job.

Anna   No.

Sammy   You said working as a doctor has made you numb.

Anna   I didn't say that –

Sammy   You should definitely quit.

Anna   I – can't.

Sammy   Why not?

Anna   That's not important.

Sammy   I didn't tell Becca.

Anna   I know. It's not a secret.

Sammy   So, why don't you want to quit, then?

Becca *comes back.*

Becca   You had a good chat?

Anna   Yes. We did. Didn't we?

Sammy   Anna is going to help me write my personal statement.

Becca   Oh, yeah?

Sammy   Yeah, I've barely started and she said she'd give me a bit of a hand getting going.

Becca   Great. I got you a coffee.

Seven

Hospital. **Anna** *and* **Meredith** *in* **Meredith**'s *office. Another windowless room, no idea of the time of day.* **Meredith** *looks absolutely knackered.*

Meredith   Anna, how was your birthday?

Anna   Fine, thanks.

Meredith   That's good. Your hair is looking lovely and shiny today.

Anna   Thanks. I washed it.

Meredith   Great. You must have brilliant conditioner.

Anna   Yeah.

Beat.

Meredith   Anna, I wanted to apologise.

Anna   Ok.

Meredith   About the other day.

Anna   Right.

Meredith   I was a bit short. And I wanted to apologise.

Anna   Yes.

Meredith   I shouldn't have been so pushy. I'm sorry. I've let things run away, it's all been very stressful and I think I was a little –

Anna   It's fine, really.

Meredith   No, it wasn't fine. Very bad, actually. I shouldn't have spoken to you like that. I was unpleasant. I stayed up all last night thinking about it, it was very unfair. You must think very badly of me.

Anna   No.

Meredith   You must. I'm sorry. Did you have a nice birthday anyway?

Anna   Yes, it was ok.

Meredith   Did you get a cake?

Anna   Yes.

Meredith   Was it nice?

Anna   Yes.

Meredith   What flavour?

Anna   Carrot.

Meredith   Delicious. You know, it's true what I said, it's so nice to have someone I can rely on around here.

Anna   Thank you.

Meredith   I think you're doing such a good job. Coping so admirably. We need more doctors like you. Do you know what you want to do?

Anna   What do you mean?

Meredith   With all this, would you want to be a consultant?

Anna   Do you think I would be able to?

Meredith   You've got all the right material.

Anna   Thank you, that means a lot.

Meredith   It's a very satisfying, very rewarding job. It's seen as a very macho thing, but I've never let that bring me down. I've always been able to keep up. I think you can keep up too.

Anna   That's really nice to hear, thank you.

Meredith   You don't want to have children?

Anna   I – I don't know.

Meredith   I have a son, you know?

Anna   I didn't know that.

Meredith   I do. We don't really know each other very well, do we?

Anna   No. How old?

Meredith   Sixteen. Teenager.

Anna   GCSEs. That's a bit of a hard time.

Meredith   He's not in school at the moment. He's in accommodation, has been in accommodation, it's a very good one. Have you ever visited assisted living?

Anna   Yes.

Meredith   It's very good, the best there is, best around here, anyway. I'm visiting him this weekend.

Anna   That's nice.

Meredith   What I want to say is, it's just worth thinking about, it's all worth having a think about, planning ahead, you know. And I can help, if you'd like, if you'd like my support you can absolutely have it. If that's the right, you know, path for you.

Anna   I'm still figuring it out.

Meredith   Of course. Doors all open, everything possible. The patients like you immensely. I read the feedback you got the other day, that young man was delighted.

Anna   Yes.

Meredith   Very complimentary. I used to have patients leave their number for me all the time.

Anna   Yes.

Meredith   All the time. Did you call him?

Anna   No.

Meredith   You're single aren't you?

Anna   Yes.

Meredith   I wouldn't have judged you. I suppose he might have been ugly, was he ugly?

Anna   Is everything alright, Meredith?

Meredith   Yes, all absolutely alright.

Anna   Are you sure?

Meredith   I – I don't much like carrot cake, actually. That was a lie.

Anna   Meredith?

Meredith   I'm not much of a sweet-tooth, really, but it's nice, isn't it, the ceremony of it, getting a cake, being given a cake, it's nice. My ex-husband was a bit of a baker, actually, used to bake, nothing too special, but for birthdays, birthdays, mine, Damon's, he'd sort of bake little things, and, you know, it's nice, iced thing, blow out the candles, sing a bit, make a wish and all that, special, makes you feel sort of special, sort of, loved, doesn't it, and I don't, no, I don't think I could tell you the last time anyone got me a cake, no, couldn't tell you, couldn't say, and, as I say, I'm not much into sweet things, but, well, not to be able to remember, not to be able to, well, that's a bit, a bit, I'm

Meredith *is crying.*

Anna   Meredith?

Meredith   Yes.

Anna   Meredith, what's wrong?

Meredith   Nothing's wrong.

Anna   You're crying.

Meredith   I don't think I am.

Then, quite suddenly, **Meredith** *collects herself.*

Meredith   So, you'll be in this weekend?

Anna   What?

Meredith   This weekend? So, I can go? I need someone experienced.

Anna   I don't understand.

Meredith   I'm going to see Damon. I need someone to cover for me.

Anna   Is that what this is about?

Meredith   What do you mean 'about'? I'd be so grateful. They're very good but the visiting hours are so complicated. If it's not this weekend, then, well –

Anna   Ok. Fine.

Meredith   That's brilliant. Knew I could count on you.

She goes before **Anna** *can say anything.*

She lies down.

And then:

Eight

David *has just finished giving* **Anna** *head.*

Anna   You're really good at that, you know.

David   Thanks.

Anna   How did you learn to get that good?

David   Practice.

Anna   Do you want to . . .

David   I'm ok.

Anna   Ok.

He kisses her.

Anna   What was that for?

David   I don't know. I wanted to kiss you. I want to kiss you.

Anna   Thanks.

David *starts getting dressed.*

David   This weekend?

Anna   I'm working this weekend.

David   I thought you weren't.

Anna   Yeah, I am now. I could see you after, though, after my shift?

David   For sex?

Anna   Yes.

David   I just wanted to be clear, what we were doing.

Anna   What are we doing?

David   Nothing. What's the worst thing you've ever done?

Anna   What? I don't know.

David   You've done something bad at some point?

Anna   I'm fucking someone I met at the hospital, that's quite bad.

David   Outside the hospital, there's a difference. What's the worst?

Anna   Why?

David   Just answer.

She thinks for a moment.

Anna   You know apples?

David   Yes.

Anna   In Waitrose there are two types of apples, gala and pink lady, and the pink lady costs 15p more, well, I buy an apple basically every day and I always put a gala apple through at the self-checkout but you know what it really is?

David   A pink lady.

Anna   A pink lady. Exactly.

Beat.

David   Do you think I'm boring?

Anna   What?

David   Or stupid?

Anna   No.

David   I'm not that stupid, you know.

Anna   I know.

David   I don't mean to sound insecure.

Anna   You don't.

David   But I just worry a bit that you might think I'm stupid.

Anna   I don't.

David   I'm a good listener, you know.

Anna   I know.

David   With my job, I'm a good listener, and generally.

Anna   I know.

David   You can talk to me about stuff, you know.

Anna   Ok.

David   So, what's the worst thing you've ever done?

Beat.

Anna   I once ran over a dog. That was quite bad.

David   Are you lying?

Anna   No. It's true. What's wrong? Why do you want me to –

David   You're always somewhere else.

Anna   Am I?

David   Yes. You are.

Anna   I don't think I am.

David   You're always off there with me, your mind's buzzing somewhere else.

Anna   Is it?

David   Yes.

Anna   David, to be honest, you hardly know me.

David   I know. It's true though, isn't it, a bit, isn't it?

Anna   You're a really nice guy.

David   Thanks.

Anna   But my job is pretty all-consuming, I miss *everything*, I am an emotional mess quite a lot of the time, I have a lot of work just looking after myself and washing my clothes and shaving and I've stopped doing that now, as you'll have noticed . . .

David   I'm not asking you to put more work in.

Anna   Right.

David   Just open up.

Anna   I don't think you understand. I don't want to. That takes energy, telling you about my emotions takes energy, telling anyone takes time, it's boring, I don't want to.

David   That's pretty arrogant.

Anna   What?

David   Sorry.

I just think it's pretty arrogant of you to assume that you know what other people will think of your feelings, that you can predict everything everyone's going to say all the time. You can't, you don't know if it's boring. You're basing that on the idea that if you talk about your feelings, people will take a lot of time to understand, when actually maybe they, maybe you should give people a bit more, well, you know, well, credit. Sorry.

Anna   I was on a road trip, it was a holiday, after I finished my third year, I had a break and I went to California and drove down the whole of the state, and it was great and I went on my own and I'd never travelled on my own before, and my mum didn't want me to go, but on the last day, I felt really happy and free and like I'd really accomplished something and then on the way back to the hire car place, I just, hit this dog. I didn't see it and then it was in the middle of the road and it made this thunking sound when I went over it, quite loud, I think it was quite a big one, I don't really know types of dogs, but, and I didn't stop to look because I was late but I guess it died, it must have died, which is quite . . . I don't sleep. At all.

David   What?

Anna   I take sleeping pills every night to sleep. I can't sleep.

David   We've slept together.

Anna   I didn't. I pretended to have slept but I didn't. I don't. I try to go to sleep and then I shut my eyes and I just can't. My mind just won't, I just go over and over everything, all the ways I, all the things I got wrong, all the people who looked at me that day and were just like, you disappointed me, you did a bad job, you're the reason why my –

David   What?

Anna   Nothing.

David   What is it?

Anna   You don't want to hear it.

David   I'm not squeamish.

Anna   I don't want you to have to – I don't want to think about it. Anyway, probably everyone feels like that? Everyone feels like they're shit at their job sometimes.

David   Most people sleep.

Anna   Yeah. They do.

David   How long?

Anna   About nine months. I moved to this job about nine months ago.

David   And it's stressful.

Anna   It is, yeah. Very. Very stressful. So fucking stressful. And obviously, everyone knows the NHS is fucked but. Right now. With everything. And I'm. You know how sometimes your mum would look to you a lot like she hated you and wanted to bludgeon you to death because you were being an absolute brat, but then would say to strangers how much she enjoyed being a mum? It's like that, basically. I like being a doctor but I'm slowly growing to hate the sight of sick people. Which is probably the most horrible thing I've ever said. Fuck. I can't believe I just said that. I.

David   I hate everyone who calls the bank. All of them. Everyone. And I have their addresses. And sometimes, I think about going over to their houses at night, and, well, I wouldn't murder them, but maybe I'd go in while they were sleeping and just move their furniture around, so that when they wake up, they'd freak out and think they were going mad.

Anna   You're funny. I don't think you're stupid.

David   I want you to be able to talk to me.

Anna   You really are a good listener, I feel like I was just talking for about four days!

David   No. It's nice. I like listening to you.

Anna   I don't hate my patients.

David   I know.

Anna   Honestly, I like most of them, some of them.

David   I know.

Anna   I'm normally much nicer.

David   You're amazing. I think you're amazing. I know we don't know each other that well, that long, but I am completely in awe of you, I think you are possibly the funniest and kindest and cleverest and –

Anna   You forgot fit.

David   Fittest person, I've ever –

Anna   Thank you.

David   You're welcome.

Anna   You're really nice too.

David   Thank you.

Anna   Generous.

David   You're bad at compliments.

Anna   That's true.

David   But you can trust me. You can talk to me. I'm not freaked out. If it helps.

Beat.

Anna   My –

Beat.

My mum died.

Long pause.

I talked to her a lot. She helped me a lot. She supported me with my work. She really wanted me to be – She thought I was a great doctor – She spent so much energy helping me and now. I just feel like. I feel like I'm just failing.

Beat.

God, I'm being so boring.

David   No.

Anna   The thing is I'm fine. I'm actually fine.

David   You're not fine and that's fine.

Anna   You sound like a tea towel.

David   Are you upset? I'm sorry if it's –

Anna   No. I'm actually not.

David   You can feel upset.

Anna   I know. I know that. I feel sad that my mum is dead.

David   That's totally understandable.

Anna   Ok. Was that open enough for you?

David   Yeah. Thanks for trying.

Anna   That's funny, what you said before, moving their furniture, that's funny.

David   Yeah.

Anna   And I don't think you're stupid.

David   You did.

Anna   Yeah, I did, yeah.

David   You feel better?

Anna   Sure.

David   You don't feel worse?

Anna   No.

He kisses her.

What's the worst thing you've ever done?

David   I'm not sure I'm comfortable opening up about it.

Nine

Anna *in hospital.*

Anna   Bye. Yes, you too. Yes. Ok. Bye, Dad.

Right. Here we go again.

Hi.

You want.

No.

No.

No.

I'm sorry.

I'm sorry.

I'm sorry.

I'm sorry.

I'm sorry.

I'm sorry to say

You have

A yeast infection

An eye infection

A burn

Oh

I'm sorry

A lovely baby!

You're a

You have

Do you think?

Cancer.

Brain damage.

Stroke.

Very little hope, unfortunately.

Ow

Bloods.

X-ray.

Bloods.

Dizzy. Stroke.

I'm sorry.

We're very busy.

I'm sorry but you just have to

Ow ow ow

I'm sorry about the wait.

I'm sorry we kept you.

I'm sorry you're out here.

I'm sorry to say.

I'm sorry.

I'm sorry.

I'm sorry.

Yes.

Don't worry

Yes, he bit me but only a little bit

Yes.

But it's fine

A little bit of blackcurrant jam on your cheek, that's all.

I'll ask.

I'll have to ask.

I'm sorry

Herpes.

Surgery.

That must have hurt.

I'm sorry.

I'm really sorry.

I'm so so sorry.

This is going to sting a bit.

It's just.

A small model of Napoleon lodged in your vagina

I'm sorry.

Your brother.

We don't prescribe.

I'm sorry.

I'll refer you.

We'll just.

Please.

I tried to.

I'm trying.

No.

Please.

Yes, Napoleon like the emperor.

Please don't shout.

Sorry.

Please stop shouting.

No, I can't

Yes.

I know but

That's not the way it works

I'm trying.

If you don't stop then

A kidney infection

No

I'll have to

I'm trying

It's fine

It doesn't work like that

I'm sorry

Please

I'm sorry

No.

I'm trying to help

It's not

I'm going to call security

My fault

No

No, thank you

Please stop

Please.

Please

stop

Please

Stop

Please

Stop

fucking

shouting

at

me

please

A burn?

Oh.

Straight into:

Ten

Anna *just entering a clinical room.* **Janet**'s *shocked to see her, tries to calculate the distance to the door, realises she can't leg it.*

Anna   Mrs . . . Oh. Oh. Mrs Sampson?

Janet   Mrs Oliver. Oliver.

Anna   It's nice to see you again.

Janet   I didn't expect you'd be the same . . . the same person.

Anna   No.

Janet   I didn't expect that.

Anna   Well, here we are. You've got a burn?

Janet   Yes.

Anna   On your leg.

Janet   Yes. I dropped the iron.

Anna   You dropped the iron?

Janet   I dropped an iron.

Beat.

By accident.

Anna   What's your real name?

Janet   Mrs Oliver.

Anna   Really?

Janet   Honestly. I mean, Mrs Sampson was bollocks, but this one's real.

Anna   I had security look for you, you got away quickly. I was worried about you.

Janet   Is the burn ok?

Anna   Did it hurt?

Janet   Of course it hurt. It's a burn.

Anna   And how are you doing generally?

Janet   I'm fine.

Anna   I've been very worried.

Janet   I'm sorry I worried you. I didn't mean to worry you.

Anna   It's ok. I'm glad you're alright. I'm glad to see you again.

Janet   This really was an accident. I had an accident. I was just ironing and I dropped the sodding thing, I wasn't concentrating. Really, honestly.

Anna   I believe you.

Janet   Thank you. I've actually been feeling much better.

Anna   Really?

Janet   Yes. I have. After I saw you I talked to my family. My daughter is a nurse, you know.

Anna   She is?

Janet   Yes. You do a great thing.

Anna   Thanks.

Janet   I'm so proud of her. She's wonderful, amazing really, so caring.

Anna   I can imagine she is.

Janet   Such a good support. She was very good and she said, right, Mum, we're going to the GP, we're going to nip this in the bud. It's really all thanks to you. I'm so sorry you had to worry, but really I'm doing ok. Apart from this stupid thing.

Anna   I'm glad you're feeling better.

Janet   I caused such a lot of fuss. She was so upset, my daughter.

Anna   I'm sure she just worries about her mum.

Janet   She's got enough to worry about. With her work and everything. Such a lot. Everything is very very hard, isn't it?

Anna   It is.

Janet   It's everywhere at the moment. It gets to you, doesn't it, no slack anywhere, nobody. It's all so, well, you know.

Anna   I know.

Janet   I'm sorry I worried you. I really didn't mean to be a bother.

Anna   It's not a bother. It's what we're here for. What did your GP say?

Janet   Really helpful. Really listened. Chewed her ear off. She was only supposed to give me ten minutes, guess how long I talked for?

Anna   I don't know.

Janet   Must have been forty-five minutes by the time I got out of there. She must have been thinking what a boring old coot, banging on about all her problems. But that's what you need, really, isn't it?

Anna   Sometimes. I'm sure she didn't think that.

Janet   Well, God bless the NHS, eh.

Anna   Yeah.

Janet   I'm really doing so much better. I think I'm going to be ok.

Anna   That's really good. I'm really pleased.

Janet   My face when I saw it was you again. It must have been such a picture. I could have screamed.

Anna   You didn't look very pleased to see me.

Janet   No. It's nice to see you. You were very nice. I'm honestly so sorry I ran out. I just panicked.

Anna   Is everything ok with your husband?

Janet   No. Not at all. He's awful.

Anna   What's the matter?

Janet   Well, I told you last time, he's a fucking golfer.

They laugh.

Anna   I'm really glad you're getting the help you need.

Janet   Yes. Trying. It's tiring isn't it?

Anna   What is?

Janet   Everything. But, we carry on. My name is Janet, by the way. Janet Wilson.

Anna   Nice to meet you, Janet. I'm Anna.

Janet   Anna.

Anna *holds* **Janet**'s *hand. Or maybe the other way around.*

They sit like that for a moment. Holding hands quite sweetly, **Janet** *has her eyes closed.*

Then, **Anna**'s *phone rings.*

Anna   I shouldn't really have that on, sorry.

Janet   You can take it, I feel alright, I'll wait. I won't run away this time.

Anna   No.

Janet   Go on, you should, honestly, I don't mind.

Anna   Sorry.

She answers. Straight into:

Eleven

Anna's *dad's house.*

Anna   Sorry. I'm here. I came, I'm sorry, there was traffic, I'm. Is he awake?

Becca   He's in there.

Anna   Ok.

Becca   He's dead.

Anna   What?

Becca   He's dead. He died. You missed it.

Anna   I –

Becca   Don't.

Anna   I –

Becca   Don't.

A long pause.

Anna   I don't feel anything.

A long pause.

Becca   Right.

Anna   I feel numb.

Becca   You're in shock.

Anna   Fuck.

Beat.

Are you ok?

Beat.

Becca   No.

A long pause.

Anna   He loved you. He did.

Becca   He loved us.

Anna   I rang him. Yesterday.

Becca   That's nice.

Anna   He only talked about you. And the baby. He was so happy.

A pause. **Becca** *looks away.*

Anna   What?

Becca   Nothing.

Beat.

It was too early, I shouldn't have told people.

Anna   Becca. I'm so sorry.

Becca   You should go in and see him.

Anna   Will you come in with me?

Becca   No.

Anna   What's wrong?

Becca   Nothing.

Beat.

You should have come to see him.

Anna   I couldn't.

Becca   I know. But you should have.

Anna   It was a complicated relationship.

Becca   Yes. I know.

Anna   I miss Mum.

Becca   Your dad just died.

Anna   I feel nothing. I can't feel. I don't feel anything. You could stick something in my arm and I wouldn't feel it.

Beat.

Becca   What did you say to Sammy?

Anna   What do you mean?

Becca   She's been talking about going travelling all of a sudden? What did you say to her?

Anna   Nothing.

Becca   I asked you to be positive. She's seventeen.

Anna   I know. I –

Becca   Go in and see him.

Anna   Please come with me.

Becca   No.

Anna   Will you hug me?

Becca   No.

Anna   Please.

Becca   No.

Anna *binds* **Becca** *into quite an unpleasant hug.*

Becca   You should go in.

Anna *is left alone and then:*

Twelve

Anna *and* **David** *at a pub.*

Anna   Hi.

David   Hello.

Anna   Can we just go to yours I'm so tired.

David   What happened?

Anna   Can we go, please.

David   Ok. Are you ok?

Anna   No.

David   Why?

Anna   Can we go to yours? I really don't want to be here. Now. We can talk in a bit but I just.

David   What's the matter?

Anna   I should have cancelled. I meant to cancel, I didn't mean to be here, but I got in an Uber and I was on my way, because this is the pub we said we'd meet at to chat, and now I'm here and I just really don't want to be, so.

David   Shall I get you a drink?

Anna   No.

David   You're being a bit.

Anna   What?

David   Nothing.

Anna   No. What?

David   Forget it.

Anna   No. What am I being?

David   Nothing. You're not being anything.

Anna   Can we go, please. I'm sorry, it's been quite a bad. I'm fine.

David   You're not.

Anna   No. I'm not. I'm really tired. I want to sleep. With you there, then we can talk. Please.

David   We'll go to yours.

Anna   You live right here, don't you. I don't care if your flat is shit, I just need to sleep. I need to lie down.

David   It's a complete mess, I'll get us an Uber.

Anna   Please, David, I just, please.

David   We can't.

Anna   Why?

David   I was going to say something a bit ago.

Anna   About what?

David   My brother-in-law. Who . . .

Anna   Hit me. Yes?

David   At the hospital. He's I think. Because I'm young or something, I guess, you assumed he was my sister's husband. But – thing is – I'm married.

Anna   What?

David   I'm married. I have a wife.

Beat.

Anna   Ok.

David   It's not. I'm not in love with her.

Anna   Ok.

David   I'm in love with you. I think.

Anna   Ok.

David   I'm going to leave her. I've been planning, it was too
. . . I . . .

Anna   Ok.

David   I'm sorry. Really sorry. I tried to say.

Anna   Ok.

David   Please say something.

Anna   Ok.

David   Other than ok.

Anna   Leave her, then.

David   What?

Anna   Leave her, leave your wife.

David   What do you mean?

Anna   Call your wife now, tell her you're going to leave her.

David   Can we just talk for a second?

Anna   Call your fucking wife, then we can sort it all out,
we'll go on a nice holiday or something.

David   I can't do that.

Anna   Why not? If you love me.

David   Don't.

Anna   You were planning to leave her, you want to leave her, apparently, you said that, so leave her.

David   This is so hard for me. I'm so sorry.

Anna   This must be a really difficult conversation for you.

David   I'm sorry.

Anna   If you get upset, David, I will punch you square in the throat. I promise.

David   I love you.

Anna   I thought you'd gone already, why haven't you gone.

She tries to leave the stage but:

Thirteen

Anna *and* **Meredith**.

Meredith   Anna.

Anna   Yes.

Meredith   Shut the door.

Anna   Ok.

Meredith   Are you alright?

Anna   Yes.

Meredith   This is difficult.

Anna   What is?

Meredith   Something difficult has happened?

Anna   What?

Meredith   There's been a situation, there's a bit of a difficult situation.

Anna   What is?

Meredith   A patient.

Anna   Who?

Meredith   You know the A40?

Anna   The road?

Meredith   Yes. It cuts through Acton.

Anna   Right.

Meredith   I live in Acton, near Acton.

Anna   Right.

Meredith   Do you know it?

Anna   No.

Meredith   There was an accident last night.

Anna   A car?

Meredith   Suicide. A patient you treated. They ID'd a burn.

Beat.

You saw her, apparently.

Anna   I – Yes.

Meredith   You did all the right things.

Anna   I referred her.

Meredith   You did.

Anna   I – I –

Meredith   Do you need a second?

Anna   I don't know what to say.

Meredith   It's very unfortunate.

Anna   Yes. What happened?

Meredith   She died.

Anna   But what happened, do you know?

Meredith   A truck. Quick.

Anna   When?

Meredith   After you saw her. There'll be an investigation. But I'll support you, you did everything right, I checked the notes.

Anna   Her daughter came to get her.

Meredith   She left the house later on. No logic to it.

Anna   I – She was –

Meredith   Very sad.

Anna   Can I go now?

Meredith   These things are very hard.

Anna   Yes.

Meredith   I'll see you tomorrow. New day tomorrow.

Anna *hasn't gone.*

Meredith   Are you alright?

Anna   I don't know.

Meredith   Very sad.

Anna   Do you feel sad?

Meredith   It's very sad.

Anna   Can we talk about it?

Meredith   About what?

Anna   I don't know.

Meredith   About what went wrong?

Anna   Yeah?

Meredith I'll defend you absolutely. You did everything right.

Anna That's not what I mean. I –

Meredith Sometimes things don't go our way, that's the way it is.

Anna How do you feel?

Meredith I feel fine.

Anna I don't know how to feel.

Meredith It's a very sad accident.

Anna But she was, I saw her, and now, I can't just, I don't know what I do now, what do I do?

Meredith The thing is, Anna, to do this job we have to build up resilience, we have to be able to separate other people, the pain of other people's pain, from our own lives. We have to. You know that. I think?

Anna How was your son?

Meredith Fine.

Anna You had a nice weekend?

Meredith Yes, thank you.

Anna What happened? What did you do?

Meredith This and that, you know. Damon was very happy to see me. And the dog.

Anna *tries to leave the stage, but:*

Fourteen

Anna.

She picks up her phone.

She rings someone.

No answer.

What's the time?

Is time passing normally? It's night, but also day?

She sits at a table on her own.

She watches something on her phone.

It's skipping.

Bright colours.

The light is shifting.

She puts her phone down.

She tries leaving the stage.

She –

She –

She tries leaving the stage.

She fills a glass of water.

She takes a pill bottle out of her pocket.

She opens the bottle.

She takes a pill.

She sits down.

She stares out into the audience.

A phone rings somewhere, but it's not hers: is it in the audience?

She stands up.

She takes another gulp of water.

She takes another pill.

She stares out into the audience.

She pours all the pills out of the bottle into her hand.

She looks at them.

She puts them back into the bottle.

She changes her clothes.

She tries to leave the stage –

She looks at the information on the pill bottle.

She googles.

She puts her phone away.

She takes her phone out.

She turns off her phone.

She pours the pills out into her hand.

She counts them.

She takes another pill.

She takes a big gulp of water.

She takes two pills and a gulp of water.

Two more pills.

Three pills.

Two more.

Two more.

Two more.

Two more.

She counts the pills left in her hand.

She sits down.

She stands up.

She puts the remaining pills back in the bottle.

She –

She fills the glass of water.

She drinks the whole glass of water.

She looks at the empty glass.

She –

She breathes deeply.

She –

She closes her eyes.

She looks ahead.

She looks ahead.

She looks ahead.

She looks ahead.

What time is it?

She looks ahead.

Just this.

She looks ahead.

For a long time.

For a very long time.

Just this.

What time is it?

She looks ahead.

Darkness.

A wailing sound.

A siren.

Running.

Footsteps.

The sound of a dog.

Breath.

Darkness.

Darkness.

A feeling that it is over.

Fifteen

Sammy *sits on the grass in the garden. It's night, but it's kind of warm. Global warming, maybe. She's vaping.*

Anna *emerges.*

She sits on the grass too. A brief pause. They take in the outside air. Then:

Sammy   Do you want to go back inside? It's pretty cold.

Anna   Did you call Becca?

Sammy   Not yet. Are you ok? Do you want to talk?

Anna   Thanks for coming to get me.

Sammy   That's ok. They've been staying at your dad's house sorting the, the funeral. They left me here, so, I got the call. I suppose they were trying to get Becca but . . .

Anna   Thank you.

Sammy   Do you want me to call her?

Anna   No.

Sammy   You're going to have to tell her.

Anna   No. Sammy.

Beat.

Sammy   Ok. Do you want to talk?

Silence.

Anna   Have you made any more decisions about uni?

Sammy   No. Not really. My application goes off next week, so . . .

Beat.

To be honest, I think maybe the only doctor I know attempting suicide might have to be a factor in my decision-making.

Anna *laughs.*

Sammy   Not sure. I could do other stuff.

Anna   Like what?

Sammy   Marine biologist. Look at fish.

Anna   That's a great idea.

Sammy   Think I'm going to go travelling. Grow up a bit first.

Anna   Can I come?

Sammy   Sure.

Anna   I'm joking. Don't worry.

Sammy   You could use a holiday.

Anna   That's true.

Sammy   Do you want a jumper?

Anna   I'm going to go in a minute. You should get one, if you're cold.

Sammy   I'm alright. You could stay? She'd want to know.

Silence.

Anna   Have you got a boyfriend?

Sammy   No.

Anna   Girlfriend?

Sammy   I wish. I'm not as interesting as that. No. You?

Anna   No. No, I don't, no.

Sammy   You should never fuck a banker. I did say that.

Anna   Very wise.

Sammy   Was that who, did he, find you?

Anna   Yeah.

Sammy   And he left?

Anna   Yeah.

Sammy   Bankers.

Anna   Yeah.

Sammy   The doctors were nice.

Anna   Yeah.

Sammy   Apart from one of them. Total prick.

Anna   Some of them are. Might have been having a bad day.

Sammy   Seemed like he didn't want to be there, to be honest.

Anna   Some of the happiest doctors I know are also absolutely the worst. Think it's probably if you're able to just treat it like any other job, maybe. Or . . . Don't know.

Sammy   There's probably a correct level of selfishness to achieve.

Anna   What do you mean?

Sammy   If you use yourself up, if you let yourself be used up, you're no good to anyone. Sometimes it's good to be selfish, it's not bad to need things.

Anna   I'm not sure you can be too selfless. Not if you've signed up to help people.

Sammy Sometimes being kind is more complicated than just looking after people. Kindness is about difficult choices; about caring in difficult ways.

Anna That was a very wise-sounding thing to say.

Sammy It's from my personal statement.

Beat.

Anna I think maybe you'd make a really good doctor, you know.

Sammy You think?

Anna With the NHS, there's nobody there to look after you. You just need to know, what you're in for, that you have to look after yourself.

Sammy Good advice.

Anna Or be a marine biologist, that's a good idea too.

Sammy Nah. Fuck the fish.

She offers **Anna** *the vape. She vapes. Maybe she coughs a little. They laugh.*

Sammy Did you mean to . . .?

Anna No. I didn't. No.

Sammy Ok. So –

Anna I'm sorry you had to come get me. That's not right.

Sammy It was pretty shocking.

Anna I'm sorry.

Sammy I'm not saying that to make you feel worse. I just. Are you upset?

Anna No. No. Are you ok?

Sammy Not really. But I'm glad you're ok.

Anna I don't know. I feel – I feel – I'm really, really tired.

She is crying. **Becca** *enters.* **Anna** *sees her and stops crying.*

Sammy   I'm sorry. I lied. I called her.

Anna   Becca, I didn't mean to.

Becca   To what?

Anna   I didn't –

Becca   It's ok, Sammy. Thank you for calling me. Your dad's inside.

Sammy *waits for a nod from* **Anna** *and then exits.*

Becca   So.

Anna   Yeah.

Becca   So.

Anna   You already said that.

Becca   Did you ask her not to call me?

Anna   I was waiting. I needed. I was going to tell you. Are you angry with me?

Becca   Yes.

Anna   Right.

Becca   I am, yes. I know that's not the right thing to say but I am. I would never have forgiven myself.

Anna   I know. I –

Silence.

Becca   I love you. More than anyone else in the world. I don't know what else to say. I love you. I love you. I love you.

Anna   I think I'm going to quit my job.

Becca   I think that's such a good idea.

Anna   I called Dad, the night before he died, and I told him I was thinking of quitting being a doctor. He said, 'Your mother would be very disappointed.' Do you think that's true?

Becca   He shouldn't have said that.

Anna   It's true, though.

Becca   I bet there are loads of things you do that would disappoint Mum.

Beat.

She didn't like your hair all that much.

Anna   I'm really sorry. About everything. This was not – I didn't really – I'm sorry about the baby.

Becca   It's ok.

Anna   It's not.

Becca   It will be ok.

Anna   Yeah?

Becca   We will be ok.

Anna   I'm so tired.

Becca   Close your eyes.

Anna *closes her eyes.*

Becca *holds her.*

And finally.

Anna *rests.*

Acknowledgements

With thanks to:

Giles Smart and Ellie Byrne at United Agents.

Lucy Morrison at the Royal Court, who read the very first mess of a draft and had the patience to talk to me about it.

Brilliant Blanche, for her care and kindness and attention, to, oddly, placed, commas.

The cast: Catherine Cusack, Jasmine Blackborrow, Hayley Carmichael, Lewis Shephard, Leah Whittaker, LJ Johnson. Man alive! What a bunch of people. What a gift.

The production team: Nadine Renny, Nancy Poole, Seb Cannings, Andrew Edwards, Greg Clark, Natalya Scase, Lara Mattison, Rachael Finney, Sophie Coke-Steel, Prema Mehta, Ben Cowens, Laura Curd, Josh York, Male Acucci, and particularly Aislinn Jackson, for delivering me a box of tissues during a particularly grim rehearsal.

Gill Greer, Adam Brace, David Luff, Eve Allin, and the Verity Bargate Award readers and jury. Their support for the play made it happen.

Dr Matthew Roche, who read the play after a week of nights and corrected my medical terminology. To Map Perry for her encouragement and friendship.

My incredible friends and my wonderful family. Every good joke in here is nicked from one of them; their kindness is the heartbeat of the play.

Lucy Thackeray, Aly Spiro, Rosie Wyatt, Oliver Wellington, Jessica Rhodes, Tom Foskett-Barnes, Georgia Bruce and Sam Ward.

Finally, I started writing this play because my sister Dr Tamsin Ellis was thinking about quitting being a doctor. She'd had enough. It's important to say that the story of the play isn't about her – the play is a fiction; I made it all up, I promise! – but the original impulse was inspired by a good person, a good doctor, feeling that there was no way to go on.

Doctors aren't superheroes. They are flawed and human and they feel afraid and bewildered and wrung-out by work, just as we all do. But unlike the rest of us, medical professionals have to see terrible things and then go home and try to be normal. We would rather not confront the day-to-day realities of how it feels to be expected to shoulder and live with experiences that no one could not be shaken deeply by, and just carry on.

The play is, in a sense, a love letter to those people. People throughout the NHS, whose startling compassion I could never hope to emulate. It is also a plea that we begin to reckon with the ways society is currently failing them. A doctor takes their own life every three weeks in the UK. That statistic should disturb everyone whose life the NHS touches – which is, well, all of us.

And while the play is not about my sister and she is not Anna, it would be remiss of me not to credit Anna's goodness, her deep desire to do a good job and her intrinsic love of other people, entirely to my sister Tamsin.

I dedicate this play to her.

Nathan Ellis